# THE WORLD TO COME

# THE
# WORLD
# TO
# COME

by *Robert W. Gleason, S. J.*

Sheed & Ward · New York

© Sheed & Ward, Inc., 1958
Library of Congress Catalogue No. 58-5886

IMPRIMI POTEST
> Thomas E. Henneberry, S.J.
> > *Praep. Prov. Neo Eboracensis*

NIHIL OBSTAT
> John R. Ready
> > *Censor delegatus*
> > May 15, 1958

IMPRIMATUR
> ✠Robert F. Joyce, D.D.
> > *Bishop of Burlington*

Burlington, May 17, 1958

Manufactured in the United States of America

# CONTENTS

Grateful acknowledgment is made to the editor of THOUGHT for permission to reprint here the chapters on death and hell, which had first appeared, in substantially their present form, in his pages.

# THE WORLD TO COME

# 1

# LIFE, LAW and LOVE

There is a disquiet at the heart of Christianity that is not found in other religions. This is so precisely because of what Christianity is: a religion of love. Inasmuch as the Christian vocation is a call to a transformation that is not partial but complete, it is a call to a self-donation that is never completed. At the very center of the Christian life there is a continual call to surpass one's present state and to give a more radical return of love to Him who has first loved us. It is this continuous movement within its very center that in its psychology sets the Christian religion apart from any other religion.

Moreover, the very essence of our religion demands this dynamism. For love tends by its very nature to go to the infinite in two dimensions, the dimension of union and the dimension of generosity. Hence the man who has understood his Christian vocation also understands this restlessness planted in the depths of his relationship with God. Where there is love no limit to giving can be appointed. There can be no "sufficient measure." Love does not divide up obligations into the necessary and the extra.

## THE LIFE OF LAW

It is of course not easy during the halting days of our slow spiritual growth on this earth to realize adequately the central role that love holds in the Christian life, and for this reason the lives of many Christians are not played out at the loftiest level of their faith. Not a few Christians appear to live at what might be called a pre-Christian level of thought. They conceive their relations with God less in terms of a personal dialogue with One who has unreservedly involved Himself with them, than in terms of law, obligation, obedience. The result is a Christian moralism. All unconsciously these Christians adopt a somber juridical attitude, and we sense its leaden atmosphere pervading their approach to the entire sphere of religion. There is a perennial human temptation to recolor God's own revealed portrait of Himself from the forbidding palette of pre-Christian theology. Luther, in his earlier writings, protested against just such an attempted deformation, and Pascal, too, reacted in his own vigorous fashion against a similar misconception. He particularly feared that those who conceived God as a sort of embodied law would, by the very processes of logic, erase the law of love so fundamental to Christianity.[1]

The truth of the matter is that God has chosen to reveal Himself in Christianity as Love, and that revelation is revolutionary. It is not, indeed, a truth totally beyond the reach of reason, yet unaided reason seems, in fact, never to have grasped it. Nowhere in the subtle pages of pre-Christian classical philosophy will we find a line to match the limpid depths of St. John's tranquil phrase "God is love." For Plato love is the child of plenty and of need, and since the gods have no needs, they know not love. Aristotle, for his part, thinks of God as the unloving cause of all love, the impersonal magnet drawing all reality to himself in an upward sweep that is necessary but without the freedom of love. Plotinus does not openly confront the possibility that God may love, although once indeed he seems to hint at it. Not a single voice in ancient philosophy, therefore, is raised in protest when we are told that God cannot love.

Yet, St. John takes it quite as a simple fact not only that God loves but that His very essence may be defined as love. The precise law of His being is love. Moreover, there is within the Trinity a necessary, hypostatic expression of love. God, in fact, loves by necessity of nature, and the necessity, the depth, the constancy of this love are reflected in the fact that there does exist at the level of personality He whom we call the Holy Spirit, substantial Love. All this the Christian has known by his faith. At the General Judgment this truth will be manifest to all, asserted beyond any doubt.

It is clear from this revealed truth that the Christian is invited to rethink his relationship with God in terms quite

different from those of any pre-Christian thinker. The disclosure that God is Love is centrally important in itself
and crucial for us. God Himself has suggested that we no
longer think of our relationship to Him in exclusively
juridical terms—in terms of law, obedience, obligation—
but that we rethink law in terms of love.[2] This may actually be said in a double sense. Law in Christianity is both
an expression of God's love for us and a clear plan laid
down for a return of love on our part.

In the Christian dispensation it has become possible to
grasp the meaning of law with a depth of comprehension
undreamt of before. We are invited to penetrate the meaning of an obligation all the way until we see for ourselves
that it is actually an expression of God's love for man. In
eternity, every law will at last be recognized as an objecti-
fication of God's love for us. The souls at judgment will
realize that at the center of every command issuing from
on high is the free personal offering of Himself that God
has embodied in the law.

If the Christian has grasped this fact while on earth,
then he has understood that it is his vocation to protest
against the universal tendency to depersonalize things.
Christians are called to repersonalize law and to visualize
it as the disclosure of God's love for them individually.
For each law is precisely that—the expression of a free
personal position that God has taken up towards us. The
very heart of that position is best expressed by the term
love. Hence the Christian should realize that he is moving
towards an encounter with God each time he is confronted
with a call to obedience.

There is, however, a psychological difficulty in realizing
this relation of law to love during this life. Its root is in

the fact that the soul is naturally reluctant to accept wholeheartedly this basic love-relationship between itself and its Creator. Between finite being and the Infinite Being there is an abyss that seems unbridgeable. This abyss is experienced by man as an anguished sense of inequality.

Perhaps the only remedy for the dizziness that shakes the human spirit contemplating the bridge of love between its personal being and the Infinite is a realistic metaphysics of grace. Unless it understands that grace establishes in the order of being a quasi-equality between man and God, the soul can hardly be expected to seize realistically the immense implications of God's revelation. There is, then, an inescapable tendency in earthly life to substitute for the categorical affirmations of revelation a series of "as if's" and "as it were's." The effect of such devices, even if subconscious, is to dilute the sobering demands of personal love on our part and the insistent affirmations of God as well into a sort of "analogical love" which is so highly "spiritualized" as to be almost volatilized. The soul, in fact, does not easily accept the premise that it is the object of an infinite love. It fears, perhaps, the dissolution of its individuality under the intensity of such a gaze.

The ordinary individual is fearful of the integral demands made even by human love. Love is such a total sort of word; it would be more comfortable if it could be whittled down into *like* or *cherish*. Hence there is for the Christian on this earth the recurring temptation to treat God as a rhetorician when He speaks of His love for us, an instinctive urge to empty the word *love* of its full significance when it is used of our relationship with Him. The word love is too global in its implications for man's life; obedience is a less total word than love.

Now at Judgment the revelation of God will be accepted in its full implications. It will be clear that if the Christian was loved, he was also called to love. No lover is indifferent to a response from the one loved. Reciprocity, or at least the desire for reciprocity, is implicit in the nature of love. God is not indifferent to my response.

What gives courage to the soul to respond more and more adequately to the demands of divine love is the fact that it is loved before it is called upon to love. Moreover, since love is an individual affair, the soul realizes that God fully comprehends all its difficulties in giving any kind of adequate response to His love. Love always takes place between individuals. It is an affair not of masses of men but between persons. The lover has some kind of intuition, even in human love, of the unique individuality of the person who is loved. As a consequence the human lover views even the defects of the beloved in the light of this love. They are seen as marring the true image of the beloved, but they do not alter the fact of love. In its relations with God the soul comprehends that it is seen by God with all its history and all its defects, but it is seen as an individual soul, as a concrete, historical, unique individual, and is loved as such. There is obviously no danger of His suffering from an illusion of love. He loves the individual as he is, and this is the fountainhead of the courage the soul needs to respond to God's love with ever increasing totality.

On this earth we are called upon to believe by faith in this love: at the Last Judgment we shall experience it as a reality. We now know that God has summoned each by name, and invited us to a supernatural destiny. In inviting us to that destiny He has revealed a love incomparably

more generous than human reason could ever have suspected. He has equipped us with a share in His divine
nature so that we are elevated in being and action to the
plane where we can respond with a love of friendship to
His love for us. As St. Jerome remarks, "Friendship either
finds two persons equal or it makes them so." God has
revealed that grace lifts us to a plane where we are
enabled to respond to His love with the love of friendship.
Since He did not find us capable of friendship, He made
us capable of it by His loving grace which confers that
quasi-equality needed before one can love another as
friend. The awareness that God has infused the gifts of
grace and charity into the baptized soul precisely to equip
it for a return of His love invigorates the Christian as he
tries to live up to the exigencies of a love-relationship in
which one partner is the Infinite God. How well he has
responded will be the subject of the final interrogation,
which, St. Matthew tells us, is to concern itself with
charity.

## THE LIFE OF LOVE

It is evident from a revelation of this sort that a whole
new atmosphere should pervade our moral life. Christianity moves in a climate completely penetrated by this new
revelation of love, and the Christian should rise to a life
compatible with this climate and not retreat to the spirituality of the Old Testament.

St. Paul is perhaps the most outspoken in his condem-

nation of those who would conceive their relationship to
God exclusively in legal terms, in terms of obedience to
law. He is never tired of reminding us that in Christianity
God has not substituted a new law for an old law. He has
not substituted a law for a law in that sense at all. Instead of a code of laws the New Testament offers us a
principle of life, sanctifying grace. Not a new and more
perfect law but a life-principle. Christianity is not a system
of laws, an ethical code, a philosophy, but a love. The
Christian is not only enfranchised from the Mosaic law;
he is exempt from law as law, from law conceived as an
impersonal, objective, self-sufficient code.

The disciple of Christ is therefore not one who knows
the law but one who lives by the life of the Master. The
law has become, as it were, an inner principle of life and
growth. The law is merely that which reveals the pattern
of life and development to the Christian. It is an objective
expression of God's loving concern for our growth, and it
is an invitation or plan for due return of love on our part.
The entire ethics of St. Paul is consequently reduced to
one principle, love of God and of our neighbor. This
Christian pattern will stand forth for the whole of humanity on the Last Day when its evidence will irresistibly
impose itself.

In conferring His grace upon us Jesus has realized the
ideal of every lover—to share in the very life of the beloved,
in the very being of the beloved, and the great law of our
supernatural being is a command to open ourselves to an
increase in that life and the love which pours it out.
Whatever fosters and develops this life of love within the
soul is commanded or counselled; whatever destroys this
life is forbidden. The Christian is thus free from all purely

exterior constriction by virtue of this interior principle that seeks its own expansion and growth. In the theology of St. Paul all the virtues are thus an expression of the supreme law of love.

St. Paul is, however, very clear on the point that freedom from the law does not mean freedom to sin. If we have received a call to liberty from the law, we have not been called to make this liberty a pretext for license. The Christian vocation is not an easy vocation precisely because the demands of love are total. St. Paul can legitimately compare the liberty of the Christian to a slavery, for it is a liberty that appeals unceasingly for a further transformation in Christ, for a more complete self-giving, destined to culminate in the life of eternity.

In contemporary literature we hear a great deal about man's metaphysical aloneness and his anguish. Man, we are told, is an aimless creature cast into being with no purpose save the development of his own liberty in opposition to all other liberties. In such a picture frustration, aloneness, anguish and insecurity seem to be his natural lot. But for the Christian, insecurity is swallowed up in the radical security which flows from divine love. Confronted with the lived truth of God's enveloping love, anguish gives place to hope, aloneness to communion. The Christian who has understood the meaning of God's advances understands his own situation in a wholly new light. The inner restlessness of his spirit is a translation into human terms of the inevitable dynamism of a religion whose law is love. Its disquiet brings no anguish but rather effort and hope. The Christian is aware that God's appeal for limitless generosity has been preceded from His side by a limitless love—a love so determined upon a response to itself that it has invested the creature with the power to respond.

The consummation of the world will thus lay bare the roots of Christian history in an unparalleled fashion. What was suspected before will be seen in its full reality in this moment of Judgment. God will be revealed in all the unity of Power, Truth and Goodness, and His love will be known in all the details of its salvific plans for man. There will be no escaping the truth that God is Love and that His judgment upon our actions and the sentence He passes is itself a testimony to that love. Heaven, purgatory, hell all testify to the unchanging fidelity of God in love. The capacity of man to receive that love determines his destiny.

# 2

# SIN

It is impossible to understand adequately the meaning of the scriptural revelation concerning man's after-life as long as we do not appreciate the tragic reality of sin in his present life. Because man is drawn from nothingness and held in being by the creative and conserving power of God he owes obedience to this source of his being. If he refuses it, he is involved in sin. Sin is not some imperfection in man's nature: it is a free, deliberate turning from God to a creature. It is simply a transgression of God's law.

This is the fundamental element that determines the seriousness of sin. God's will is the sovereign law which all creatures must obey. Irrational creatures fulfill it perforce, but the liberty of man is solicited by God through

His law. Sin as an affront against the all-powerful, all-merciful, all-just personal God is very clearly traced throughout the whole of Scripture. But it is doubtful if modern man has a very strong sense of this element in sin.

It is true that man today is very well aware of the personal nature of the offenses which may impair the relationship of friendship or love. But unfortunately he does not always realize that the bond which unites him to his creator is just such a relationship: one of love with all the obligation of fidelity which this implies.

## THE MEANING OF SIN IN THE OLD TESTAMENT

The Old Testament is at pains to make clear that what is of supreme importance in human life is the will of the Lord. This is the highest and holiest form of existence; and man must strive with all his energy to fulfill this demanding will of Yahweh, despite any personal sufferings it may cost him. Because man is the heart of universal nature he submits to this universal natural law of Him who has created nature.

But he is required to submit freely. God has involved Himself in man's history by creation. For through it He has submitted Himself, as it were, to human freedom, since the good which He intends for men cannot be evolved without the free collaboration of His creatures. God will solicit, He will lure, He will attract, but He will not compel men to seek their own good. The tragedy of man, which constitutes his ultimate seriousness, lies in his fearful capacity of hurling a free *no* at His Lord.

The Old Testament theology of sin constantly stresses this notion of sin as a direct offense against the Creator. David's adultery, for instance, displeased God Himself, and David acknowledged that he had sinned against Yahweh in offending his neighbor. Frequently, indeed, the Old Testament calls sin an apostasy, precisely because God had linked Himself to this people with the understanding that they would obey His laws. To attack these prescriptions was to attack the good estate of Israel, since the Law was the loftiest sign of God's presence among His people.

Sin is sometimes also described in a general way as fornication; but perhaps for the modern mind the most shocking image is the Old Testament metaphor of sin as marital infidelity. Because God had chosen to make Himself the spouse of Israel, sin was equivalent to adultery.

The image of idolatry is often assimilated to adultery in the Old Testament precisely because the relationship between God and the people of Israel could not be expressed in the purely juridical terms of a testament and bond. It needed to be interiorized in terms of mutual love. All this is forcefully dramatized in the story of Osee. Osee pursues his unfaithful wife with a persistent love which seeks her return from prostitution to himself. So it is that the sin of Israel is not only a rebellion against God and a rebellion against the testament God has made with His people, but it is a drama in which Israel rejects and wounds the marital love of God for His people.[1]

This notion of marital love naturally carried with it the

Old Testament conception of a jealous God. At times this notion of jealousy suggests God's "anger," but at other times it is translated simply as "grief," the grief of a loving husband confronted by the infidelities of his wife. Doubtless the love of God for Israel is a demanding and exclusive love, but it is also supremely genuine love. It is because of His love for His people that the anger of God descends upon the enemies of Israel, and from it arises the punishment which He inflicts upon the sinner. It is because God loves His erring people and the erring sinner that He pursues them and punishes them that they may return to Him.

The sin by which man takes leave of God in an insulting fashion does not destroy the transcendent divine majesty, but it does turn man, the beloved of God, away from His first and saving love. The concept of divine jealousy does suppose God's rights over man, but these are the rights of a loving husband towards an unfaithful wife: a husband seeks for the return of his unfaithful wife not merely in order to proclaim his right but in order to enjoy her love and her presence in peace.

It is not easy, in fact, to give a precise description of the Hebrew concept of sin because of the wealth of connotations that this concept carries with it. Underlying some words used for sin is the notion of an attempt against the very life of God. In the Genesis account of Cain, in the story of the Deluge, in the history of the doom of Sodom, we feel in sin this evil gesture which rebels against God and which seeks as it were to take His life. This brings to the fore the entirely personal quality of sin which the Old Testament never fails to stress.

The frequent treatment of sin as a missing of one's aim underscores the Israelite notion of sin as a lie and a deceit.

Sin means a failure to fulfill that ultimate relationship to the person who is our goal: God Himself. We are bound to God by indissoluble ties, which sin refuses to respect in its attempts to wound the term of the relationship, God. Of course when one misses one's aim it is not God who is wounded. To fail to attain God is simply to fail to attain what man wants, by the law of his nature, more than all things. It is failure to fulfill one's own destiny. There is a text in Proverbs which expresses this idea in human fashion. Wisdom speaks and indicates that he who fails to obtain wisdom ruins himself: "all those who hate wisdom love death." This is an apt description of the sinner's state when he fails in the fundamental aim of life. He is embracing death, he is courting nothingness. To sin is to lose one's self, to lose one's heart, to fall from the way. The English word *fault*, in fact, suggests this notion.

Sin is also a rebellion, a revolt against the law of God and a transgression of His rights. This idea of the transgression of the rights of the other involves for the Old Testament mentality a general notion of the hostile position which a sinner adopts toward God, as though God were in fact the enemy. But this is also a direct revolt against the divine design for men, because God intends to bring us to our complete development through the fulfillment of His laws. The interior state of the sinner is therefore described in the Old Testament as one of heaviness; the sinner is burdened by his own injustice. Sin has something unbearable, intolerable about it, and it imposes upon the conscience of man an insupportable weight.

We can perhaps learn something further about the nature of sin as the Old Testament mind viewed it if we examine God's reaction to it. Frequently the word "irritate"

is used to describe this reaction. This implies that sin stirs
God to anger, or more accurately, to sorrow. In Jeremias
we are told that the Israelites have followed other gods
and have provoked God to wrath or grief. The Hebrew
word therefore suggests that the intention of the sinner
is actually to invade God with his own sadness, if this were
possible.

The basic concept here also enfolds the notion of aversion from God, together with a certain contempt or offen-
siveness. Sin is thus an evil *for* man as it is an evil *against*
God. The sinner launches himself against the commandments of God with the weapons of his scorn. In some
genuine sense, therefore, he attempts to offend and wound
God Himself. Among the pagans sin was sometimes
thought of as an action which actually destroyed the divine
transcendence. This notion finds no place, of course, in
the revealed religion of Israel, in which it is clear that
although sin is aimed directly against the Creator, yet it
redounds to the injury of man alone. The sinner offends
and wounds God only because he wounds one whom God
protects with His love, one whom God has chosen for His
family.[2]

Sin also attacks that covenant between God and His
people which the Old Testament described as a bond of
salvific, marital love, founded in the Lord's free choice
of Israel. By the sin in Paradise Adam and Eve were deprived of the divine friendship. The serpent persuaded
them that God was a selfish tyrant who did not have
their true interests at heart. And this primitive element
of distrust of God is persistent in the Israelite notion of
sin. Adam and Eve thought that they would become as
God, capable of establishing the moral law for themselves.

By sin they manifested their distrust of the altruistic love of God for them and behaved as though they believed Him a selfish lover. So also in Israel the sin of idolatry particularly offends God because when Israel seeks after other gods she proclaims her distrust in Yahweh as a loving protector.

The Israelite is well aware that man is sinful; in fact he has a profound and introspective consciousness of the universality of sin. Because of the great distance between God and His creatures and because of the spotless purity of God, all creatures come to sense poignantly their sinfulness before their Creator. No one can claim absolute purity for himself. The psalmist pleads with Yahweh not to judge his servant, because no living person can appear just before God. If Yahweh is to keep alive the memory of misdeeds, who will remain standing before Him? This consciousness of sin, even when a man cannot recall a definite transgression, doubtless gave rise to the idea that some of the suffering experienced in this world is a punishment for sins forgotten or not clearly recognized. Man is frail and he is subject to many temptations; it is impossible that he should come to the end of his life having conquered all temptations with equal success.

The Jews always have this profound sense of universal sinfulness. Indeed, in some sense men are sinners because of a mysterious solidarity in evil. For Israel it was Israel herself, the nation, which was the classic sinner. The individual was assimilated to this collective entity of Israel in his sin. It was the whole people who had turned against God and who would return to Him again in repentance; and the individual return was to follow this general pattern, the great return of Israel herself. For as the people have sinned, the people are the first to suffer from the innumerable communal betrayals of God. When the Prophets emphasize the responsibility of the individual in sin they are also intimating that the individual is responsible for the destiny of Israel insofar as he is a part of Israel. The great adulterer is the nation; and the individual sinner resumes, with his personal transgression, the attitude of Israel herself, who is unfaithful to the faithful love of Yahweh.

This sinful rejection of God implies that one makes a choice between God and the creature and finds God wanting. This is the subject of the complaint of Yahweh. God slowly educated His people to a constantly more interior concept of sin and to a constantly more individual concept of their responsibility. In the Old Testament is shown not only a keen awareness of the sinfulness of man's deeds but a consciousness too of the sinfulness of the human heart in its deepest thoughts and desires, and these sins of thought are forbidden in the same fashion as sins of action are forbidden. God preserved the just man with a clean heart. Gradually the Israelite learns to distinguish between the purely ritual and legal prescriptions of the law and the moral prescriptions. Gradually he learns to understand the distinction between the evil intention and the objectively evil act; he slowly learns to see sin as an attack upon the mutual relationship of love which exists between him and God.

Throughout the Old Testament, however, the Jew sees the punishment for sin as a suffering to take place in this life. It is only very late that God brings the Jew to understand that the true works of life are spiritual and that the punishments due to sin will fall upon man most heavily in

the next life, just as the rewards for virtue are not so much
the rewards of this life as they are of the next.

## THE MEANING OF SIN IN THE NEW TESTAMENT

The New Testament continues and marvelously expands
this movement towards interiority. Jesus openly opposes
the pharisaical concept of sin as a purely exterior transgression of the law. The Pharisees had insisted so strongly
on ritual purifications that they were in danger of leading
the people to a purely exterior religion. In opposition to
them Jesus continues the work of the Prophets of Israel
in insisting upon individual interior responsibility. Sin is
a product of the evil will of man and it comes forth from
the heart, from the evil thoughts and evil will of man far
more than from the formal exterior deed.

Much can be learned from Jesus' statement concerning
sin, but even more from His treatment of sinners. He
makes it clear that sin is universal, that at the end of the
world men will be divided into two opposing camps; but
He also makes it clear that His purpose in coming is to
redeem man from sin. His treatment, for example, of those
who sin by weakness is extremely gentle and tender. He
condemns those who sin against the light, He condemns
those who refuse to accept the gift of salvation that God
has sent in Him, but towards the sinner in the ordinary
sense of the term Jesus remains infinitely compassionate.
When the Pharisees accuse the woman taken in adultery
Jesus befriends her. In the house of Simon the Pharisee

He defends the sinful woman. He chose Zacheus the publican to be His host, and He engages in long and open conversation with the adulterous woman of Samaria.

His teachings in the various parables have been a source for Christian reflection on sin and have molded the Christian attitude from the very beginning. One should be noted especially: the great parable of the Prodigal Son. The remarkable thing which strikes us at once is the joy of the father upon the return of his son; the center of the entire narration is the father, and it is with his psychology that the sacred author is chiefly concerned. From the parable it is eminently clear that sin is directed against God. The son declares, "I have sinned against heaven and thee," and his sin has consisted above all in his willful departure from his loving father. The necessity for conversion is made clear here, but what we should note above all is that the father is more anxious, more genuinely concerned, to receive the son than the son is to make his return. The father has been keeping watch for his son, full of anxiety and longing for his return. It is he who runs to greet the prodigal while he is yet a long way off.

The sinner who seeks reconciliation with God does not, therefore, long for reunion with one who detests him but with one who is already with love awaiting his return. It is not God who must change His mind and His attitude towards the sinner, but the sinner who must change in his attitude towards God. God demands of the sinner his sincere repentance, and demands it absolutely, because man is free and as he freely turned from God, so must he freely return. But his repentance will be welcomed with love and joy.[3]

Our Lord also reminds us that those who are called are

not automatically saved. One must work to attain eternal life. The road is narrow and there are many ambushes. The Christian is engaged in a continual struggle with Satan during his life. What is required above all is obedience to the law of God in charity. This new law of charity which Jesus proposes is certainly far more demanding than the Mosaic law, because it penetrates more deeply into the very heart of man. The commandments of God are thus clarifications of the one great commandment of charity. Christian morality will constantly insist upon this interior love of God, and in the light of this insistence one can see again, from another point of view, that sin is a defection from the demands of the interpersonal love between God and man.

From the way in which Jesus deals with them it is also clear that certain physical evils and the phenomenon called possession manifest somehow the enslavement of sinful man to the power of Satan. Jesus is engaged throughout His public life with a struggle against Satan, the great adversary of our human nature, and man is engaged with Christ in this struggle. It is all too clear from the Synoptic Gospels that sin is not external failure. It is the free refusal of man to serve God and his free choice of rendering this service instead to Satan, who then obtains a certain control over the sinful man.

The Gospel of St. John further develops this notion of sin in the New Testament. We note first of all in John that Christ's major task is to take away sins. The chief contribution of St. John to the theology of sin consists in this: that he reveals sin as a hatred of and an aversion from God; Jesus, who is one with the Father, is totally and eternally divorced from sin. "Who is there who shall con-

vince Me of sin?" Jesus is the light of the world, and the
sinner is in darkness and seeking darkness. By sin man
opposes his will to the will of God and thus cuts himself
off from the God who is love subsistent, according to the
Johannine definition.

Instead of being the servant of the Lord the sinner becomes the servant of sin and the son of Satan. The sinner's
father is Satan, and he wishes to accomplish the will of
his father. He who commits sin is from the devil, and the
devil from the beginning was a liar and the enemy of the
human race. The devil from the beginning stood outside
the truth; he deceived Adam and Eve, and he has continued to deceive the human race. In Christ is the truth;
in Satan are lies. Christ has eternal life; Satan is the prince
of darkness and of death. Satan moreover is a murderer.
It was he who introduced death into the human race, according to the Genesis recital and the book of Wisdom.
He bears mankind a great hatred, and he tries to arouse
hatreds within the human race as he succeeded in doing
in the case of Cain. He who does not love, St. John declares, remains in death. He who hates his brother is a
murderer, and we know that a murderer has no part in
eternal life.

The Jews, in the Johannine sense of those who would
not accept the light, preferred to dwell in darkness. Because their works were evil they hated the light. The sins
of the Jews revealed their hatred of God; and this hatred
was made manifest in their rejection of Christ. The Jews
who rejected Him, said Our Lord, had no excuse for
hating Him, they hated His Father. The advent of Christ
has revealed this inner hatred of God at the core of sin,

and the great Johannine contrast between light and darkness is followed up by this contrast between hatred and love. All the Johannine Epistles manifest God as the God of Love. The great commandment, the new commandment, is the commandment of love, and he who fulfills this commandment toward God and his neighbor manifests the life, light and presence of God within himself.

Everywhere in the writings of St. John one finds this drama of sin and redemption as the contrast between light and darkness, between death and life. The saving Lord comes as the word of God, as the light of life to restore men to the light, to draw them out of darkness and to give them eternal life. But among men is the sinner: one who refuses to accept the gift of God. Sin is not only a transgression of the divine law but it is also a refusal to accept the gift of life. The sinner prefers the passing goods of this world to the eternal life of God. By his revolt he no longer owns the title of Son of God; he becomes a son of Satan, a liar in Satan's image. Johannine theology likes to emphasize the languor and sickness of soul which sin reflects and which in mortal sin becomes actually the death of the soul.

St. Paul's dramatic personal experience of his own moral weakness convinced him, the converted Pharisee, of the universality of sin in all men, both Jew and Gentile. St. Paul personalizes sin as though it were a great world power dominating the whole of humanity without Christ. Sin is like an evil interior force awakened into action by contact with the Mosaic law. The law, while good in itself, lays bare this factor of sin within man, since it reveals what must be avoided but does not give the power to man to escape doing it. Man is conquered by this interior domination of sin and finds himself divided against himself.

St. Paul has given us an admirable description of the state of the man who takes joy in the law of God according to the interior man but finds another law in his members at war with the law of reason. Sin appears in Pauline theology as a master who dominates his slaves: we have all been sold into slavery by sin, and it is only the coming of Christ which will deliver us from this tyranny. Sin dwells within us, in our sinful flesh—that is to say, in our flesh insofar as it has become an instrument of sin. It is only Christ who will restore to the sinner the Christian liberty.

The opposing slavery was introduced into the world by the transgression of our first parents, and it uses the flesh as its instrument for domination. Paul states most strongly that this power of sin pervades the entire human race and that without the assistance of Christ man can never conquer it. Only by a certain death and resurrection is sin overthrown, a death and resurrection by which man is assimilated to Christ dead and resurrected. The sacrament of Baptism, which joins us to Christ's death and resurrection, transforms our entire being as Christians. What we are required to do is to adapt our psychology, the mode of our action, to this new Christian mode of being.

The law of Moses shows us this interior force of sin in all its deadly power just as the serpent was shown in the Garden of Eden in his true colors as a murderer. The Holy Spirit is opposed to this internal drive of sin, and between the two there is a constant strife. Even in the man reborn to Christ there remains an absolute antinomy between the sinful flesh and the Holy Spirit. The flesh in the Pauline sense, with its own wisdom, is opposed to God with an implacable enmity. Sin is a power by which man is turned away from God and actively opposes Him.

Insofar as he is under the domination of sin, a man not only does not obey the law of God, but indeed he cannot obey it. The concrete transgression of the law in any individual sin is only an expression, an exteriorization, of this grip of the sin within man. The effort of God to lead man to happiness and to the complete expansion of the divine power planted in his soul at Baptism is attacked by sin. The sinner does not take anything away from God Himself, but he does diminish His exterior glory when he refuses to permit the development of divine grace in his soul and in the souls of those about him. Mortal sin deprives the soul of charity and suppresses those acts of charity which should flow from the divine seed planted within it at Baptism. God seeks the manifestation of His own goodness in the sinner, and the sinner refuses to manifest it by refusing to accept the goodness and the gift of God.

## SIN AND HISTORY

Freud had a good deal to say about two fundamental human instincts: the impulse to defend life and the impulse towards death. Certainly men are nearly as preoccupied with death as with life itself. The philosopher Heidegger even maintains that man is dedicated to death, has a genuine instinct for death. In the religious sense this is surely true, for mortal sin, the death of the soul, seems to exercise a constant attraction for man. St. Paul has pointed out this active interior solicitation to death.

If a Christian is to understand the importance and the personal meaning of his life, he must study this unhappy reality, mortal sin. Otherwise it is impossible to seize the Christian meaning of history, to grasp the tragic possibilities inherent in man's situation. As we study the march of history from a Christian perspective we cannot fail to note the contrast between the accounts in Scripture of the creation and the redemption. In the creation the work of God was accomplished with effortless joy. His almighty word called into existence the earth, the heavens and all things on the earth. Nothingness did not resist the command of this creative word.

How different is the story of the redemption. As we follow the account of God's efforts to lead human events towards the redemption of humanity we are overwhelmed with a sense of the divine labor it requires. For the whole of history is one long development of the theme of God's fidelity and man's infidelity, God's striving and man's resistance. In creating man God introduced an element of risk into His plan, because the freedom of man is ultimately a capacity for saying No as well as Yes to God.

As we follow the history of the chosen people we wonder at the patience of God. How often He has to begin His work anew, how slow is the process of educating humanity. What a marvelous inventiveness God shows in taking up a work that has been partially spoiled by the rebellious will of man and beginning again with patience and ingenuity to reweave the broken threads of His salvific plan.

From the beginning, from the first moment when God

offered a testament to Israel, it seems as though Israel had made up her mind to play the role of a stiffnecked and rebellious nation. And through it all God is faithful to His promises. At times He shows His wrath and punishes Israel severely to bring her back to the right way. The cloak of His providence extends continuously over every detail of Israel's history. Often He intervenes to show His loving intent with regard to His people. He has given them His own laws as a symbol of the compact. He is Israel's God and Israel should be His people. To what other nation has He spoken in this fashion? He gave it the Judges to instruct the people to wisdom and to form in them a sense of justice. He gave great kings to Israel to rule her and bring her to that point in history to which He was directing her destiny.

Yet, in spite of such marvelous benevolence, in every period of Israel's history, as the Prophets make clear to us, humanity betrayed God. Doubtless there were great heroes and heroines in Israel's history, but there are also great manifestations of sin. All too often Israel follows after strange gods and prefers the golden calf to the God of Israel. The great thing throughout all this period of the Old Testament is the constancy of God in the face of man's infidelity. God is generous to give when man is niggardly to respond.

Very often we meet with images indicating a sense almost of frustration in God as He deals with this rebellious and sinful people. We have the image of the solitary harvester who returns alone at eventide to his home, weary and fatigued at the effort of the day and apparently discouraged. We have the picture of God treading the wine press alone, His garments red with the stain of grapes.

Both of these are metaphors suggesting the efforts that God puts into the formation of a blameless people.

Finally we have Isaias' daring image which compares God to a woman in labor, undergoing anguish to bring forth a people worthy of the divine vocation. In order to build up the family that He wanted for Himself God seemed obliged to suffer and to labor that a Church might be born without spot or blemish. And Israel is faithless and ungrateful as she goes after strange gods and commits adultery.[4]

This history of Israel is of course symbolic of all God's relations with the individual soul. Each of us has the same history in our life that Israel worked out in her time. The reproaches of Good Friday are addressed to us no less than to Israel. "What more could I have done for you, My People?" He has said to each of us individually. The lament still goes on. To the salvific plan of God we have all preferred, at one moment or another, our own rebellious, sinful will. Israel slew the owner of the vineyard and called down His blood upon her children. We too, if we examine ourselves deeply enough, discover within ourselves the roots of deicide.

The divine labor to form another member of the Church of God, another member of the Body of Christ, goes on in us despite this. Human freedom has been called the risk of God, but when we observe God's answer to our sinfulness we cannot help but marvel at the divine ingenuity. He does not let go a work that has been spoiled by us, but He takes up the task anew, and with us as resistant instruments he builds a new covenant.

We are involved in this great struggle to form the people of God, the new Jerusalem, and even the material universe feels repercussions of this struggle within itself. For each of us sin has an intensely personal meaning; we can confirm from experience the Pauline analysis of the law within ourselves which struggles against the good. And with St. Paul we can each appeal to God, "Unhappy man that I am, who shall deliver me from the body of this death?" and to each of us God replies, "The grace of God, by Jesus Christ."

Although the mystery of sin defies a full analysis, we must study it in order to grasp our own dignity and importance. This impediment to the march of God's history, this risk of God, must be grasped in some of its human meaning; otherwise we cannot understand the full weight and meaning of our human destiny. And in order to make any genuine study of the meaning of sin we must first situate this rebellion in the dialogue between God and oneself.

God has committed Himself to a love for me personally, and He solicits my liberty to a reciprocal love. But at the same time my gift of liberty makes me capable of betrayal. Fundamentally this is the meaning of grave sin—a betrayal of love itself. Every betrayal in love is of course a betrayal of the very person who is called to love. Greater intelligibility will no doubt emerge in the course of our study, and yet we must realize from the first that there is no such thing as a complete understanding of sin, precisely because sin is not intelligible on its own terms at all.

The very nature of sin is to be a *privation* of something that is due to man. It is a privation of something which should be there. In itself it has no positive being; it is intensely negative. It is not truth, it is not goodness, it is not being, but a lack of all three. It is a defect in something which should be without defect, it is a lack of being where being should be. The blindness in the eye is a deficiency, a privation of what should be there, sight. So also sin is really comprehensible only in terms of the being, the good, the truth, which it negates. Sin is a defect of the due order the will of man should have towards the divine law. When Wisdom says in the Old Testament, "He who hates me loves death," it is expressing the essence of sin very well. The sinner puts his mouth to the fountain of non-being and drinks deeply.

Of course he does this in a gigantic illusion of grandeur, since he sees sin masked with splendor and power. Sin has myriad disguises, but in the end it is essentially emptiness where there should be fullness. It is a fundamental negation or diminution of the human being.

What we have to do, if we are to grasp this reality of sin, is to strip off its masks. Sin does not attract the human will by presenting itself as what it is but by representing itself in terms of its opposite; thus nothingness appears under the guise of greatness, weakness under the guise of power, fear under the guise of boldness. In Pauline theology sin is not conceived as evil because it is forbidden; it is forbidden because it is evil, because it turns man away from his final happiness. To think of sin as a violation of some objective law capriciously fixed by God to limit our liberty is absurd. The law of God is the preservation of my liberty, not its destruction. The law of God is a signpost pointing to liberty. We must beware, then, of erecting sin into anything like a real value, for if sin had any positive element about it, it would have some goodness, and it has none. So often sin masquerades as an invitation to life on a bolder, more active, personal plane. Yet in reality it is a refusal to live and a rejection of life. It is an existential leap in the direction of nowhere.

At its core, sin is of course an implicit attack on the attributes of God. Were its intention carried to fulfillment, sin would launch an attack on the very nature and life of God Himself. Sin is a gesture which would dethrone God as sum and source of values and put the sinner in His place. This is the ancient prevarication of Adam and Eve, who would have liked to become a moral law unto themselves. Sin attacks the unicity of God because there can be but one moral norm, one absolute goodness, and that is God. Any attempt to set the sinner up as the measure for human conduct is an implicit attack upon the unicity of God.

Nor does the wisdom of God remain free from the rebellious attacks of the sinner. In the Old Testament we have seen how sin does embody this contempt for the wisdom of God and for His providence. It is as though the sinner charged God with not understanding all the complexities of our human nature, as though the sinner charged God with having a merely abstract knowledge of what was right and fitting. It is as if the sinner claimed that God lacked the existential knowledge which took into account all the particulars of the sinner's situation. We are called upon by God to believe in His providential care over us. This was a great temptation of the Jews: to abandon belief in God's providence the moment things seemed to be going wrong for them. When God fed them with manna they accepted Him, but when exile came they rejected Him. God had constantly to teach them that His providence extended to every detail of their lives and that the sufferings He permitted had a salvific meaning for them.

The sinner refuses to accept this role of God's providence as sufficient in every situation. He prefers to think that his own wisdom is better fitted to cope with his life than is the wisdom and providence of the God who made him and placed him in this situation. The holiness of God is outraged by this because such an attitude seems to place that holiness on the same level as the virtue of man. There is no doubt that the sinner often fails to appreciate realistically the transcendent sanctity of God. And yet these attitudes are rather pathetic in a way. No normal man accepts them when they are thought out and fully conscious. Sin is much more than an intellectual opposition to God's attributes.

There is something ultimately mysterious about sin. It is perhaps best grasped as a refusal to love. It is a refusal of life itself. It is rejection of the demands that maturity makes upon us, that love makes upon us, that life itself makes upon us. God has wished to communicate to us a share in His own Divine Life, that life which we call Sanctifying Grace. He has wished to establish a most intimate union between Himself and us, a union which has physical bonds. But we, for our part, would like to sever the union with God because we fear the demands it makes upon ourselves.

A certain narrowness of vision is connected with sin, but it is deliberate in its nature. The sinner sees a part as a whole, whereas actually when we see the punishment that is visited upon sin we are quite often only seeing the whole for the first time. For being resists being dictated to and will not be dictated to by man. It imposes itself upon man, and it is useless and hopeless to confront being with a command. The natural order revenges itself upon the sinner, and it indicates to him that he has attempted to go against the very laws of being itself.

So often, too, sin is merely a cloak of sham courage,

hiding the sinner's cowardice as he retreats from that wholeheartedness which is demanded of love. He retreats before the demands that the Divine Lover makes, and he dissembles his timidity with bold words. All sorts of rational evasions are used by the sinner to avoid admitting the open fact that he is afraid to love, in this fashion, on this plane. If the intellect were left to itself in peace, it would undoubtedly condemn the sinner, but the sinner involves the intellect in all sorts of strange and devious paths to justify itself. St. John has said that he who loves not abides in death, has chosen death as his homeland. This is actually an apt description of the sinner, because sin is death pretending to be life. How many there are who turn eagerly to this death, embracing it under the pretext that it represents life.

## SIN AND PSYCHOLOGY

The major claim of sin is, in fact, this claim to be a fulfillment of man, although it is actually his frustration. We hear today a great deal of talk about repressed desires and inhibitions, but sin thwarts man at a level far deeper than the instinctive level. It foils him at the very level of his existential dynamism, at the very level of being. For man thirsts for the infinite. He could even be described as a living thirst for God, and sin parches him. Whether we realize it or not, we desire God with every fiber of our being. Sin frustrates this interior *élan* to the Infinite which is of the very structure of our self. The very nature of man as free spirit must protest against sin, for man cannot tolerate in peace this bafflement of his deepest self.

In order to avoid evil it helps to study the psychological mechanisms by which man sins, for this process which balks the longing for God is peculiar indeed. We might formulate the question by asking how a reasonable man can possibly choose nothingness and self-defeat. The activity by which man sins is a self-sabotage; it is an attack on his fundamental orientation as man to growth and expansion of his own potentialities. If it is true to say that evil is nothingness, how is it possible for an intelligent and a free being to choose it? We know that we do so, and yet we cannot lay the blame for our choice upon ignorance, since a certain degree of knowledge is required before we can sin at all. We must be aware that the action we are choosing is contrary to the law of God and therefore contrary to our own being, to our own good. We must be aware that this choice that we are making is a choice contrary to our own nature. How, then, can one consummate this choice?

Psychologists tell us that at a certain point in many neuroses, the neurotic has a personal choice. He can either step over the boundary line separating neurosis from psychosis or he can choose not to. Certain psychologists believe that man chooses his psychosis, his madness, as a defense against an unpleasant reality. Does not something like this occur in sin? We create for ourselves a state of mind in which we are estranged from reality, but our disorientation is not due to obscure mechanisms; it is due to our own free choice.[5] We deliberately choose to set ourselves outside the bounds of reality with regard to this evil choice we are about to make. Since we know that sin means self-limitation, self-destruction of our supernatural life, we cannot choose sin precisely under this aspect of evil. We must make for it a mask of good. But in order to construct this mask we must call upon our intelligence and our will to work together to deceive us and to persuade us that an apparent good is better than a real good.

Yet we must emphasize the fact that this self-deception is a free act. Were it not free, there would be no sin. What we do is tell ourselves that what the good God wills for us is not really good for us, because the good God is not really good and does not really love us. Of course, we do not go through this process consciously, since we would immediately recognize the stupidity of pretending that God hates His creatures. Is it not this very thing with which God reproached the Jews in the Old Testament? How often He rebuked them for their ingratitude and lack of trust. They acted as though they believed that God was deceiving them and only pretending to have their genuine interests at heart. This is the classic pose of the sinner; one in which he acts out this delusion of a God who is not the real God but a God at secret enmity with man. It is only in such an unreal world that we can choose as good what God forbids.

This psychological description does not make sin intelligible, for sin is not ultimately intelligible at all; it is not being. This whole process of creating an imaginary God who does not have our genuine interests at heart is a process freely begun and freely sustained during the act of sin. The experienced reality of the apparent good with all its pressing quality of concreteness seduces the mind of man, frequently in a very short time. Theologians tell us that the deliberation required for mortal sin can be had in a very brief moment. In a briefer time than it takes to describe the process, man pulls himself out of reality and chooses an apparent good which he knows is a real evil for him. To one who has appreciated to its full depth the terrible reality of deliberate grave sin, the alienation that it implies from reality, from self and from God, the question cannot but occur as to the frequency of grave sin in a human life.

## SIN AND THEOLOGY

There are many who think that theologians take a certain joy in pointing out the number of grave sins that occur. But obviously the theologian is as much shaken as is the ordinary man at the thought of this free rebellion against the creative love of God which mortal sin is. One of the great theologians of the past century, Cardinal Billot, was so moved by this thought that he came to the conclusion that there are very few subjectively mortal sins actually committed.

His reason for saying this, however, would not be particularly consoling to the majority of men. For the reason which Billot assigned for the infrequency of mortal sin was simply this: the ordinary man does not have the moral intelligence required to commit a mortal sin. Billot held that the majority of men are theological morons. They may be excellent business men and know how to conduct their financial affairs with prudence and with dispatch. But because of the milieu in which they have grown up, because of the amoral environment in which they have been educated, they simply do not have sufficient moral sense to commit a grave sin. In this theory, the education in morality required to commit oneself seriously against God would simply be lacking in most men. However, most theologians have rejected Cardinal Billot's theory. It is true that one requires a certain degree of human understanding and human intuition to commit a grave sin, but the ordinarily intelligent man should certainly have the capacity to commit himself seriously with regard to the moral law.

Other theologians lay heavy stress upon what we might call the fundamental orientation of man. Is the man under consideration one whose general attitude is directed towards God and virtue or towards self and vice? In this theory, what would count is not so much the isolated individual act of a man as the general trend of his life. Does his life manifest a tendency to satisfy self or God? What manner of man is this? What is his most fundamental attitude? Is it an attitude that longs to serve God and his deepest most genuine Christian self, or is it at variance with God and with his deepest self? Beyond doubt there are some men who, in spite of a seemingly integral life, do not seem to diffuse the good odor of Christ. They seem dominated by an inner spirit of selfishness which takes myriad forms in them without ever being so fixed in one act that one could point to a specific mortal sin.

To theologians who favor this point of view, the important thing would be an attitude of soul rather than a concrete, individual, measurable act. However, most theologians do not accept this "moral portrait" theory, because it does not seem to respect the decisive character that any one individual act may have in the formation of one's moral life. No doubt certain theologians evolved this explanation as they confronted the question whether or not a man would be condemned to the everlasting torture of hell for missing, let us say, one Mass of obligation. And we admit that their anxiety has good cause, but we do not feel that their solution is a lasting or a just one.

There are other theologians who hold that mortal sin is committed very frequently, and they appeal to the testimony of the mystics who claim to have seen souls falling like autumn leaves into hell. They also point out that the requirements for mortal sin are not so difficult as one might conceive. If one genuinely understands that the act in question is gravely contrary to the moral law and if one has the necessary freedom required for a genuinely human act, one can commit mortal sin. But perhaps these theologians are stressing more the objective aspects of sins and emphasizing less the subjective requirements for mortal sin.

A generation ago theologians tended to think of the knowledge required for grave sin as an abstract, theoretical knowledge which might be called simply the use of reason. But today theologians stress more the fact that man needs a certain type of valuational knowledge in order to commit mortal sin. A man must, in short, appreciate in some sense the value that is embodied in the law of God he is about to break if he is to commit a mortal sin. This is what Cardinal Newman would have called a real knowledge in opposition to a notional, schematic knowledge.

Other theologians admit that one individual mortal sin, as opposed to a lasting attitude, can very well merit the eternal pains of hell. But they point out that it would seem that such a sin would have to be one that engages the sinner's whole personality. It would seem that if one act is to dispose of my whole eternity, it should be an act that commits me wholly, an act that sums up all my previous experiences as man, sums up all my past, and prefigures all my future. Thus it would be an act that represents me wholly and entirely as I have arrived at this stage of my human development. Normally such a sin would seem to be rather a sin of malice than a sin of weakness. In this point most theologians would agree: that those souls who are in hell today are there not so much because of weakness as because of malice.

If we accept this theory, we could see how such a sin of malice could be prepared for by a sinner's previous sins. His previous sins could gradually adapt him to express his entire moral personality in one individual act. For an act to express the whole moral physiognomy of a man is not at all inconceivable. Those who are familiar with the findings of depth psychology are aware that a single act can have a decisive, historic importance in the formation of an individual personality. It would seem logical that if a man is to dispose of his entire future—of his eternity, in fact—he would have to have some realization that he was disposing totally of himself with regard to the infinite. It would seem that he would have to have some awareness of the meaning of God and the meaning of the act which he was about to commit.

There are other theologians who appear to hold that the only really deadly sin is the sin of making the wrong final option. Thus that final choice, against God, at the moment of death which sums up all man's previous acts and expresses his personality completely would be the only really grave sin. Such a theory, we believe, goes contrary to the entire Christian tradition, which has always held that man can commit many grave sins, meriting hell, during his lifetime. We believe that it would be dangerous to say that the only act in which man can wholly commit himself is this final option of the moment of death. It is, besides, very uncertain whether any such option takes place.

What we can say ultimately is that in order to commit grave sin a man must have some sort of interior understanding of the evil he is doing. Without some appreciation of the value which is at stake in the law of God it seems doubtful that he would have the requisite knowledge to commit a subjectively grave sin. It is true also that man only gradually reaches the adult age of his instincts. Children and young people do not ordinarily have a sufficiently developed scale of values to enable them to insert this act in its proper place in the scale of good and evil.

There are likewise in many people two registers of freedom. One is freedom from external force and the other is the truly interior freedom of choice which is at times hampered more or less, limited more or less, by the defects in the person's moral education or by the various neurotic disturbances in his personality. Without discussing such subjects as subconscious motivation, one can still realize that man's freedom is limited and variable and that not every objectively mortal sin needs to be counted as a subjectively grave sin destining its author to the eternal pains of hell.

# 3

# DEATH

From whatever point of view one approaches it, death is not a simple question. It remains mysterious, and arouses in the hearts of men complex and contradictory reactions which they seek somehow to unify. There are those who fear death and who weep at death and those who take leave of their departed ones with feasts of joy, feeling that the dead at least are escaping the common calamities of this earthly existence. Other philosophies in the past have tried to conjure death out of existence by an attitude of noble scorn, as though death were a casual incident, unworthy of great attention.

## DEATH AND PHILOSOPHY

Until the present era, however, death remained on the margin of formal philosophical speculation. An Epicurus, fatally preoccupied with the subject, could give us his celebrated quip: "While we live, death is absent, when we die, we are absent, so death is simply nonexistent for us." But it was a remark whose sincerity was belied by the brooding tenderness with which that philosopher hovered over the subject of death. In fact such a reply demonstrated its own bad faith. The attempt to depersonalize death is inauthentic, for when our death confronts us, it will be unavoidably, gravely, ours.

An occasional philosopher, such as Schopenhauer, has argued that life is an illusion from which we are liberated by death. It is a blessing to die, for death delivers us from the world of vain desire and struggle into the calm purity of nothingness. But aside from the fact that such chaste silence appeals very little to the Western mind, philosophy has no guarantee that the unmasked face of death puts an end to struggles or illusions, or removes man from conflict with the world of being and suffering. Conjugating the verb "to die" in the indefinite plural solves nothing. As Pascal remarks, "One always dies alone."

This is precisely where the mystery of death is placed by the modern mind. Historical circumstances have made the modern philosopher aware that in the domain of human experience, death is not merely an impersonal problem but a mystery which engages man's entire being, a mystery which is not only objectively thrust upon us from the outside but which we confront from within, which involves us, the subject, in its very data.

Thus, for some modern philosophers, death seems to be a demand within the person himself, an exigency so personal that only the subject can cope with it. In this philosophy a man would be dedicated to death from the beginning, and dedicated to it in the unique appearance that it will have for him alone. It would be useless for him to speculate upon another's death, for this would be to reduce death to an impersonal mode. What could possibly be the meaning of death as it is regarded in this light?[1]

If this philosophy strikes the ultimate note concerning death, then it is obvious that death is always an interruption, because man's reality, his being, is never fully possessed in this life, never realized, never rounded off the way an object can be. Therefore one could never speak of death as completing the development of man: it would be senseless to conceive death as the finishing touch of a human life, for a human life by its very meaning is activity, becoming, development. Process is of the very essence of human life. Does not human consciousness first pose itself as a liberty, a project, a choice, a development?

This movement towards transcendence of one's present state, towards realization of oneself, could not be frozen at any moment of time, because there is nothing in common between the human condition verified in each person as essentially unfixed, and the fixed completeness of an object. It is true that my states of soul and my projects suffer completion, but I myself do not. If one wishes to think of himself as fulfilled, completed in this life, then he must conceive himself as an object, whereas he is in fact essentially a subject. Since human possibilities are indefinite it is useless to talk of completion by death. Moreover, the character of death as a chance encounter forbids one to speak of it as a completion.

Nor would one, according to this view, legitimately think of death as an event that finishes life by interrupting it from without. For death is not something that is met from without; it is not merely a limit imposed on self from the outside. Rather death is inscribed within the self: I live death. It is my climate. It is the dimension of my life and consciousness. Man is prompt and ready for death from the moment he is born. His circle of possibilities has not so simple a limiting principle as this chance death coming from without. Death could not be a cessation of life due to fulfillment or the exhaustion of the possibilities of liberty, for death is really constitutive of being. From birth to death we live with the demand of death inscribed on our consciousness. Since it is precisely this reality of death which gives its authentic meaning to life, we must unravel the meaning of death in good faith and not be satisfied with interpreting it superficially. Such is one modern philosophy of death.

But if consolation is a philosophical task, we must admit that this philosophy of death is not, after all, particularly consoling. The man who faces death according to such a view will come to recognize the radical absurdity of all things; of a being cast into life to deploy his liberty against the background of the nothingness which surrounds him. He himself carries nothingness in his heart, and his advantage over other men would merely be the advantage of cynical self-knowledge. Nor could this self-knowledge take place without a certain anguish when such a philosopher recognizes his absurd human position. If nothingness in the form of death has penetrated the human situation, then the man who comprehends this fact will value very few things in life. It would be hard then to escape the conclusion that death is the perfectly absurd, casting a shadow of total absurdity over life and the universe and the entire world of values.

To maintain, then, that death is a final plunge from the nothingness of life into a nothingness which sums up man's possibilities and gives his humanity its fundamental and pathetic meaning is to limit intolerably our liberty, our very significance as man. Surely some more human attitude is possible before death.

As a matter of fact, Christianity offers a solution to the agonizing problem of death; a solution which is at once more human and consoling. Dealing with death across all of history, involved with death as chance encounter and martyrdom and murder, fitting men for death by teaching them how to live, exalting the death of the saint and receiving the dying sinner to her forgiveness;—on every stage of history, as life reaches its inevitable last act, the Church has truly been a broad and living bridge between time and eternity.

## THE CONCEPT OF DEATH IN THE OLD TESTAMENT

To transmit her living synthesis of wisdom, tenderness and courage, the Church has not failed to draw upon all the examples of history in which man has gone forth, rational, humbled and serene, to meet the Creator. Some Christians are astonished when they become aware of the almost total silence maintained by the Old Testament writers over many centuries with regard to the question of personal survival and the states after death. It seems that the thought of the Hebrews and the ideas of the modern mind on these subjects are poles apart—even the modern mind which discards religion—for in the Old Testament there is no evidence whatsoever of the preoccupation with the subject of death which is part of today's mentality. The progress of revelation in this sphere is clearly discernible: from the very imperfect truth of the Old Testament to the explicit statements of the Christian Church.

Although the Jews at certain periods did have some idea of an eternal joy held out to them, it was an idea on the margin of Jewish dogma. The Sadducees, even in the time of Christ, denied the resurrection and were nonetheless accepted as priests. For centuries the Jewish people had no belief in a retribution after this world. This may astonish us, for whom the notion of retribution seems primary in religion, but if we reflect on the content of our own belief about the after-life, we will perceive that there is a very little in it for the imagination: the popular descriptions of heaven and hell are often misleading. Hence our surprise might legitimately be reduced somewhat when we consider the Jewish attitude to death and survival.

We must note first that the Old Testament gives evidence of the same complexity of thought, the same human difficulty in explaining death, that philosophy has encountered. There are different traditions in the Old Testament on this subject, sometimes superimposed one upon the other, sometimes following one another successively.

Secondly, Old Testament thought moves in a completely different anthropological climate from ours: it had, for example, no clear philosophical distinction between spiritual soul and material body. The *ruah,* the soul, is doubtless a more ethereal reality than is the body, but except for the last centuries of pre-Christian Judaism, the soul is absolutely inconceivable separated from the body. For the period of the Patriarchs, death is, then, a very simple and human affair, a natural, normal occurrence for man as for every living thing. It is a reality that causes no problems; one accepts it from the hand of God as one accepts any other event.

No question is raised concerning the status of the man after death, for death is the normal condition of man. One can at best hope for a death that is the culmination of a happy old age. The great expectations of their people were the basis of a supernatural peace in the attitude towards death of the early Jews, the mystery of the individual's destiny being penetrated by joy in the promise of divine fullness to the community.

Yet if the dead cannot be said to survive, they still have some kind of shadowy existence. In Jewish thought the human person does not disappear completely with death, but existence continues under conditions which scarcely merit the name of life. Death is considered a sort of minimum vital state in which all the life forces have so low an intensity that the dead seem hardly to live at all.

Yet one cannot say that the departed have been absolutely reduced to nothing, because there still remains some shadow, some vague image, of the individuals who yesterday were full of expanding activity. The condition of the dead is so faint and so inactive as to resemble an exhausted sleep: still the opposition between death and life remains a *relative* one.

The Old Testament, moreover, frequently recalls the sober and peaceful death of those who fell like ripened fruit in the maturity of a rich and fulfilled old age: the Patriarchs, Abraham, Isaac, Jacob, go to their peace after a long and happy old age.

Again, when considering the Israelitic attitude toward death one must always keep in mind the continuity of their community. While the Israelite may die, the community of Israel, God's chosen people, goes on forever. What is essential is that the elected people continues. It is to the entire people, it is to the race of Israel, that God gave His Word, His promise of salvation and protection. As a consequence, the Israelite hope rests first of all upon the community, since to the Israelite the fate of the individual is not so important as the fate of the race. Nor in this view does the dead Israelite entirely lose contact with his people. In some fashion or other the individual Israelite shares in the history of his people.

In order to show how death does not mean an entire rupture of the relationships between Israel and the dead, one would have to describe the Israelite concept of a family. One notices first of all the anxiety of the Jews in regard to the procreation of children, especially males, because the male child insures the continuity of the family. Abraham, after he had been tested by God, receives as a reward for his obedience an unheard-of promise of many sons. To die without children was to the Israelites even a mark of displeasure on the part of God; and in order to assure himself of a male descendant the Israelite instituted the Leviritic law. By this law the brother of a man who dies without child was obliged to marry the widow; and the first son of this new union would be considered the son of the dead man.

Consequently, for the Hebrew, the thought that a human being continues to exist in his children is quite ordinary. Man is not an individual without any bond between himself and his neighbor, without any bond in space or in time. He makes one body with his descendants and his ancestors. The future and the past of the entire tribe are present in the destiny of each member of this chosen people. Because the Israelite realizes that he is part of this chosen community which began through the rule of Yahweh and which will reach its fulfillment through the rule of Yahweh, he has a sense of belonging to a structure which can never perish. His individual story opened with Abraham or with Adam, and it will not close until the Kingdom of God is fulfilled upon earth.

Because of this sense of tribal destiny, the Israelites accepted death with tranquillity. By so accepting its term, one shows gratitude to God for a long and productive life, a sign of God's approval. We look in vain through the great writings of Israel for a troubled curiosity or fear with regard to the eternal arrangement of things. The subject of the dying Israelite's anxious meditation seems to be not so much the future world to which he is going as the temporal future of his people.

This concern for the race and lack of concern for the individual is illuminated by the last words of Jacob and of Moses. Again, the struggle between Jacob and his brother Esau for their dying father's blessing would strike us in the light of a different religious attitude as callous indifference to a parent in agony: the sons were more concerned with their own hopes for the future than they were with the death of Isaac.

And when the plague struck all the firstborn of Egypt, the Israelites did not react with any compassion or horror, but hastened to profit by the opportunity and enriched themselves at the expense of the Egyptians. When the Israelites saw the pursuing Egyptians strewn in death along the tides of the sea they gave thanks to the Lord. On another occasion, Moses asked God to call death upon two hundred and fifty laymen who had rebelled against the priestly hierarchy: he is without pity for the individuals concerned; death is regarded as a just if severe punishment for those who rebelled against the established order of things.

So death appears in inspired Hebraic literature as a matter of comparative indifference, seldom a subject for philosophical reflection or regret. Simply, many things are more important than death. There are, for instance, the offenses against the law which were punishable by death: apostasy from God, the worship of false gods, rebellion against the priestly caste, bearing false testimony, forgetting God or prophesying falsely. The penalty of death is most often imposed for offenses which would imperil the Israelite community.

There exists side by side with this human view of death a current of agnosticism, which we find especially in the Sapiential literature. A survival in the loving memory of men seems to be the only survival worth striving for. The horizons of this life are the only ones worth considering. It is astonishing to us to read the profoundly human prayer that Job offers to God in his sufferings: he begs merely for a little rest at the close of his days so that he may at least have the joy of the hireling at the end of toil. The absence of any appeal to another world where compensation for his sufferings will be offered is almost shocking to us.

This Sapiential current is not wholly lost in pre-Christian times. Ecclesiasticus in the second century before Christ likens men to animals and declares that it is useless to attempt anything for the departed, since they are dead and destined to remain so. At times this current of thought is tinged with a certain bitterness in its reflections on death, which is not found in the peaceful resignation of the Patriarchs.

It is certainly true that there appears early in Judaic thought the somber region called *sheol,* the abode of the dead—but here we cannot allow ourselves to be deceived. *Sheol* is not restricted to the biblical tradition; it occurs in other Semitic religions. Moreover, it does not refer to anything like an immortality of the soul—which is conceived as material like the body—but is simply a vague subterranean place where souls live a rather grim life sometimes pictured as devoid even of consciousness. It is a region of darkness and silence, the land from which there can be no return, inhabited by shades entirely cut off from the land of the living. It is a jealously guarded prison, and arrival there is something to be feared, for there the praise of the Lord, in which man's dignity finds fulfillment, is eternally stilled.

This mysterious home of the dead was generally believed to be an enormous territory under the visible world. As such, *sheol* doubtless reproduces certain of the charac-

teristics of the Greek *Hades* and the *Arallu* of the Baby-
lonians. There are those who believe that the Israelites
actually borrowed their concept of the Kingdom of the
Dead from their neighbors. This, however, cannot be
verified: *sheol* is an enigmatic land; even the origin of
the word is obscure. Some Old Testament scholars believe
that it is derived from the verb "to demand," and they
explain *sheol* as the spot where the Eternal Judge demands
an explanation of his life from the dead individual. Others
believe that *sheol* rather signifies a desert place, so that
the Kingdom of the Dead would be like desolate flatlands,
without life, without order, without color. At any rate
*sheol* signifies in general fashion the abode of the dead
and evokes for us the image of a primitive world unmarked
by the variety or splendor of material creation.

How the Israelite pictured *sheol* is suggested by references in the Old Testament. At times *sheol* is called simply
"the tomb" or "the ditch," which would originally mean
a cistern. At times this cistern served as a prison or a
grave. Sometimes *sheol* is compared to the place of destruction or of perdition. Again it is called the home of
eternity, the house of the dead. The geography is always
extremely vague, but the region of the dead would be
somewhere at the extreme opposite point from the world
of the heavens; it would thus be at the lowest point of
the universe. *Sheol* is, then, a nether world of tombs and
graves, a vast cemetery under the earth, where the dead
are gathered, nation by nation, slave and master, rich and
poor, sinner and just. It is an image that will recur vividly
in the Descent into Hell of Virgil's *Aeneid,* and its tonal
atmosphere is not unlike that of Dante's *Inferno,* except
that in these great literary treatments of the afterworld

the human, the particular, the emotive connection with mortal life give a poignant universality to one's encounter with the souls there.

What is especially remarkable, in view of our retributive idea of the after-life, is that the differentiation among the dead in this kingdom does not depend upon the ethical character of the individual's behavior while on earth. It is possible that at the height of *sheol* the great ones of the earth live surrounded by marks of their earthly aristocratic rank. But in no case do we read that the fate of those whose moral life was conformed to the will of Yahweh is happier than that of the sinner. Any inequality seems to be based rather upon considerations of a ritual and social order, although some scholars have seen in the later writings of the Old Testament an evolution of the notion of *sheol* into a temporary dwelling where the dead await resurrection and judgment. In this case the souls would probably be divided into the good and the evil.

*Sheol* is Virgil's *irremeabilis unda,* a land of darkness, silence and forgetting. Ecclesiasticus tells us that the dead know nothing, they are forgotten and they have no part in the life of the living. Between the dead and the living all bridges are burned. Between Yahweh and the dead there do seem to remain certain relationships, yet the faithful Israelite feels himself abandoned in death because he is no longer able to confront his God. Not only does he miss his contact with God, but he lacks all sense of community, because he feels cut off from the destiny of his people. Death means that one will be alone, the last horror of eternal solitude. The most insupportable facet of the Israelite picture of *sheol* is doubtless this separation from the community. *Sheol* is not, therefore, simply a distant region where the departed wait piously for the resurrection; it seems rather an insatiable monster which devours Israel.

*Sheol* in fact does not merely designate a place; it is also a condition of soul. The Israelite descends into the infernal world at the moment when he dies, but even in life, misfortune comes to him as a dark foreshadowing of death. At the moment of sin, despair or failure, death shows its power. The dead can be compared to a drowned man tossing witlessly in the ocean, forgotten by all: *sheol* is associated with the destructive aspect of water.

In the Mosaic theology death is seen not only as a fact of nature but as a penal sanction for sin. This represents a completely new world of thought. When the will of God meets the resisting will of man death arises as a punishment for this transgression. The Mosaic catechesis of the Genesis recital moves in a juridical framework when it treats of death.

Western theology will prolong this perspective of death as penal, leaving to the Oriental Church the development of the idea of death as purification. Pauline theology will also stress this penal aspect. Such a juridical conception naturally hastened the development of the idea of retribution.[2]

In the Prophetic current of thought the resurrection of the dead appears first under the form of images. At first these images refer directly to the triumph of the Israelite people at the coming of the Messias and really affirm very little about death or resurrection. But with Daniel we hear a completely new and clear accent: he speaks plainly, and for the first time, of the resurrection of the dead. Here it is not the survival of the separated soul—an idea foreign to Hebrew psychology—but the resurrection of the whole man, the person, the self. It is moreover a resurrection that takes place for the punishment of the evil and the reward of the good. But even in this text Messianic perspectives are rather obscurely joined to eschatological perspectives.

After the persecution of Antiochus Epiphanius revelation concerning death and its consequences had made definite progress in Jewish thought. Ezechiel had spoken of a resurrection in a sense that may be taken to mean the resurrection of the people of Israel to power and justice. But in Daniel the fact is definite and clear: an individual corporal resurrection is intended.

Forty years after Daniel the second book of Machabees offers another important witness: it too teaches the resurrection of the body in the future Messianic age. The mother expects to find her sons again, "at the time of mercy." The sacrifice of Judas shows that in the thought of Judas and the author of the book it was useful to offer sacrifice, the purifying effect of which would be felt on the day of the Messianic resurrection. So it is evident that in the last century of pre-Christian Judaism there were those who believed in the resurrection of the body. But this belief in the resurrection of the body was by no means unanimous.

Still another advance in thought closer to our idea of the immortality of the soul comes with the Wisdom of Solomon, probably the latest book of the Old Testament. This concept is not biblical or Hebraic, but was probably derived from the writer's encounter with Hellenistic culture. He stresses the idea of a personal survival with God. At death the soul remains living and is united to God by knowledge and love. Thus the hopes expressed in Psalms

16 and 73 are resumed here in a perspective that combines Platonic philosophy with biblical revelation. It is certain that Wisdom puts the people of God on guard against any type of amoralism or doubt about the future life. Death is in some sense the culmination of the moral life and sanctions the all-important will of Yahweh.

That the author inserts these truths in a framework alien to previous biblical thought—the Hellenistic framework of the survival of separated souls—is perhaps accidental from the viewpoint of revelation. It is clear that the Old Testament closes on a certain note of tension between this Hellenistic theme of the immortality of the soul and the biblical theme of the resurrection of the dead. Further developments in the New Testament will move unmistakably in the line of the resurrection of the dead rather than the line of an immortality of separated souls. Historically the two concepts belong to two contrasting ethical and religious worlds.

## THE CONCEPT OF DEATH IN
## THE NEW TESTAMENT

When one comes finally to the New Testament, he cannot but be impressed by the certainty reigning there in contrast with the hesitations of the Old Testament. Jesus takes a resolute stand: Yahweh is the God of Abraham, of Isaac, and of Jacob, and He could not be properly called their God if He did not recall them to life. Jesus' Resurrection is the pledge of ours. At the resurrection full recompense will be given for the works of the just and the unjust alike. The final judgment concerning the moral life of each man will be given at the moment of this bodily resurrection—which is clearly reserved until the end of time.

But the doctrine of Jesus—remarkably clear upon the truth of the resurrection from the dead—is also remarkably reserved upon the condition of man between death and resurrection. We are not told what the state of the dead is nor in what their activity consists before the resurrection.

The greatest certitude that Jesus gives us concerning death is the fact of His own resurrection. From that cardinal truth, the preaching of the Apostles will join our own resurrection to the death and resurrection of Jesus. With Christianity the dominating fact is not death but the living Christ.

In Paul's theology of death there are several dominant themes. His thought is penetrated with the idea of a providentially arranged economy of salvation which has at its center the death and resurrection of Christ. Moreover, his whole consideration of death is bound up with his theology of salvation. It is principally in its connection with sin that he considers death, particularly in his earlier letters, so that his conception of death is thus closer to the penal and juridical idea of the Mosaic catechesis. For Paul the death that entered into the world as a punishment for one sin has been conquered by Christ: the coming of the Lord has radically overthrown the reign of death and has introduced the reign of life and immortality. So Christian life, in St. Paul's view, flows from the great central mystery of the death and resurrection of Christ.

Not only does the individual destiny of man enter into this plan of God for victory over death through Christ's death, but the mystery also has cosmic repercussions. Not only does the individual aspire to be liberated from death, sin, and the law, but the entire universe awaits with longing its liberation from the servitude imposed upon it by sin. For Paul the entire Christian life is but a prolongation, in the universe of men and of things, of the mystery which recapitulates all Christian reality—the redemptive life, death and resurrection of Christ.

The heart of the Pauline conception of death lies in the parallelism he traces between Adam and Christ. Both recapitulate humanity; Adam as the source of death and Christ as the source of life. Life is introduced into the world as a fruit of the justice of Christ, and the reign of death is abolished. As the thought of Paul develops over the years, the theme of Christ as life increases in depth. In Romans he refers to the groanings of nature for its liberation. In Ephesians, Corinthians, Colossians, the theme will be developed, centered on the new element that the victorious resurrection of Christ has introduced into all reality. Just as, in the intimate bond between human nature and the material universe, all creation suffered a tension between life and death, servitude and freedom, so in the end, because of Christ's victory, the entire universe will victoriously manifest the glory of Christ and of those who commune in His risen life. In Jesus the entire reign of death had delivered itself over to mortal combat with the kingdom of life and had lost the struggle. But in Christ's triumph, death, the last enemy, will be destroyed and the triumph of life cannot be arrested.

As in the gospel accounts, the Pauline conceptions of the condition of the Christian between his death and the resurrection of his body remain undetermined. His whole perspective is that of the Last Judgment, when man will rise to receive the final reward or punishment for the things of this life. Certain details of the description which Paul gives us are doubtless part of the traditional literary framework of the apocalypses of pharisaic tradition. The trumpets and the voices of archangels do not perhaps indicate the charism of inspiration to the same extent as does the great truth the Apostle is essentially affirming: "And thus we shall be with the Lord—for ever." It is already a difference of perspective from the earlier Epistles and a foreshadowing of the Johannine ideas on death.

As with so many other biblical themes the Johannine Epistles, particularly the first, and the Apocalypse, add much to our knowledge of the theology of death. St. John, preoccupied with the theme of life, accepts from the Genesis story those details which concern death as a portal to life. For St. John, Christ is the central mystery; Christ, "the Living One," whose death and resurrection affirm in an especial way His sovereign, divine life. The Christian is baptized into the death and resurrection of Christ and so shares from the beginning in His victory over death. John stresses continually the fact that this victory is already inaugurated in the possession of divine faith and grace and that the Christian, "the Conqueror" as he is called in the Apocalypse, already possesses germinally the life of the celestial city, and has already won his triumph over death. He will be rewarded with the "crown of life" by Christ, who will conduct him to the very springs of the water of life.

For St. John Jesus' resurrection has penetrated the mystery of death with the foretaste of life. Jesus Himself is the "firstborn from among the dead," possessing life in

Himself and communicating it to His own. Death in St.
John is almost never considered in itself. It is, so to speak,
absorbed in the person of Christ who in His resurrection
is the principle of ours. "I am the resurrection and the
Life" is a summary of the Johannine views on death.
Death is of only subsidiary importance, enveloped in the
life that is in Christ and in the resurrection of the Christian that is in some fashion already precontained in the
Christian's adherence by faith to Christ. The Christian
has already judged himself by the attitude he has taken
to Christ. In principle he is already dead or already living;
his temporal life has perspectives that reach forward into
eternity: man has already passed from death to life, as
his attitude to Christ, "the living One," demonstrates.

As the scriptural evidence concerning death makes
clear, death is no longer a terminal experience for man;
it is a particular episode in the development of life, an
episode which assists man in discovering the true life.
And in this sense death may, with immensely more truth,
be called a birth, a beginning of life.

On the other hand it is almost equally evident that in
the Christian framework death has been truly interiorized.
For the progressive liberation of the forces of life which
remove from death its terminal significance demand
another kind of death; unless the grain of wheat falls into
the ground and dies, it remains alone, without fruit. Death
is thus one of the earliest Christian experiences—the first,
in fact, for Baptism is an insertion into the death and the
resurrection of Christ. The entire sacramental life of man
is centered in this progressive invasion of his soul by the
powers of death that liberate the resources of life in
Christ. All the Christian life is lived in communion with

this Paschal mystery of Christ's death and resurrection.
Corporal death interests the Christian less than the advent
of the communal triumph of the Messianic times to which
his own death causes him to draw near.

It was naturally within this complete framework of
biblical revelation concerning death that the Fathers of
the Church thought and wrote. They placed their emphasis on the transformation of the meaning of death in the
light of the resurrection of Christ. Before the acceptance
of Christ, man's whole existence, body and soul, was
under the dominion of death; but since the coming of
Christ this dominion has been broken in principle. For
the Greek Fathers redemption is seen within the total
framework of the Incarnation as a healing union of human
nature with the living God who vivifies that nature, body
and soul. The Incarnation is itself radically the redemption, for by it *sarx*, flesh, has been united to the vivifying
divinity. The Redemption of the Cross is but the supreme
moment of the Incarnation. The Word unites Himself to
a mortal body to liberate within all humanity the forces
of life in order to crush the forces of death. The domain
of death is thus in principle destroyed and corporal death
is no longer to be feared—it may even be longed for as
the condition of union with Christ.

Death is thus, in fact, a crisis of growth. The Christian
will not be fully man, fully Christian, until this crisis is
surmounted. The ultimate fulfillment of the human person,
body and soul, demands this rebirth which is corporal
death. The sacraments meanwhile assist in the destruction
of the forces of death within the Christian, and the
sacraments are saturated with the light of the Paschal
mystery of Christ's death. Death has certainly been interi-

orized in the sense that Baptism, which introduced the
Christian into Christ's death, has to be an enduring influence in a man's life. The initial death of Baptism is made
effective by the mystical dying, day by day, to the destructive forces of sin.

As to the state of the Christian after corporal death, the
Fathers add little to the data of Scripture. The just
certainly enjoy happiness, but one could not say that their
happiness is in every detail complete. The resurrection
of the body is always the Patristic perspective. The
Fathers invite us to think of beatitude as a successive
development of the resurrection; and our task is to render
more precise what would be lacking to the soul before the
Parousia. This is particularly so since corporal resurrection would seem to begin in this life through the influence
of the Eucharist. But in general, the Fathers manifest the
same reserve as the Scriptures concerning the state of the
Christian after death.[3]

## DEATH AND THEOLOGY

It was only natural that subsequent dogmatic development should unfold the great biblical themes concerning
death and its significance. Medieval thought concerned
itself particularly with the elaboration of a complex theology of the states after death. Subsequent theologians
followed the lead of St. Thomas in his *Commentary on
the Sentences* and preserved in general the order he indicated there. At times, however, writers from Thomas to

Suarez devoted excessive attention to questions more curious than decisive. The theme of the particular judgment receives, for instance, an emphasis that it does not have in the sources of tradition. It was natural, too, that in the sixteenth century the tract on the Last Things should take on the polemic and apologetic tone characteristic of the theology of the period. If the biblical themes of the victory of Christ, the common triumph of the Parousia, receive less attention than the particular judgment and purgatory, this was normal in the age which stressed the importance of the individual and was much concerned with indulgences, remuneration and the fate of the soul immediately after death.

What has been of greater interest to modern theologians is not so much the state of individual souls after death and before resurrection as the experience of death itself, the meaning of which engages a major portion of modern theological thinking on the Last Things. The separation of body and soul, the passage of the soul to heaven, hell, purgatory or limbo: such would have been the summary account of the medieval theologian. But today's theologians prefer to explore the idea of death on more speculative grounds.

The consideration of death as an especially decisive moment in human life is, of course, not a recent development in theological thought. Certain theologians in the nineteenth century had defended the concept of a sort of special illumination at the moment of death. Some thirty years ago a theory was proposed which gave the moment of death an altogether decisive significance; it was suggested that at that moment there was granted to the soul —even the soul of the unbaptized, apparently—a final

option made by virtue of a special illumination from
eternity. Numerous other theologians have recognized the
unique import of this moment of death and have granted
to it some special significance. Often these theories are
particularly concerned with the problem of the salvation
of unbaptized infants. What is of interest here is less the
origin of the various speculative theologies of death, concerned as they often are with one or another particular
problem, than the theology itself which they elaborate.

Many modern theologians begin from the central idea
that the mystery of Christ's death is the pattern for the
death of the Christian. But the death of Christ was an
exceptional and decisive act from many aspects. The
redemption of mankind was accomplished by a death that
was from the beginning freely consented to, freely desired,
freely accepted. It was indeed imposed from without by
the executioners of Christ, but it was at the same time
freely willed and accepted by Christ in advance, and at
every step of the way. The oblation of the sacrificial
Victim was accomplished in the hushed privacy of the
Upper Room before the executioners, perhaps, had even
been apprised of the necessity of this death.

It is undeniable that to one who confronts death in an
impersonal way, the death of Christ, like every other
death, seems an event which was suffered rather than
chosen. To the witnesses of the death of Christ, despite
the magnificently free utterances which summed up his
interior attitudes on the Cross, His death must have appeared as something submitted to rather than something
elected, as passive rather than active. And the attitudes
of the Apostles in the days succeeding His death demonstrate that even their perceptive eyes had seen nothing

in the crucifixion except suffering endured. For they were probably accustomed to thinking of death in its ultimate stages as a passive, not an active, experience—a falling asleep in the Lord, to awaken to Him on the other side of death itself. In death thus understood, the liberty which had characterized and, as it were, constituted the man would have been suspended while the person underwent an experience in which his deepest self had no part.

Such a concept of Christ's death, however, would deprive the supreme redemptive act of its share in the conscious liberty indispensably required that the redemption take place at all. It is not entirely certain that the experience of human death, and especially the death of Christ, need be entirely similar to the unconscious death of other living organisms. There is at least a restricted sense in which we can speak of death as an act, an activity freely chosen. Thus, for example, death and resurrection in sacramental Baptism certainly involves a principle of death interiorized in the person and active throughout his life. The death referred to and intended in Baptism is a mystical and not a corporal death. But it does involve corporal death in a sense. The Christian who commits himself to the providential plan for his life in all its intimate particulars doubtless accepts both the laws of nature that govern and determine the moment of his bodily dissolution and the decisions of God that support and determine the application of those laws. His acceptance of the order and situation in which he is divinely placed is, in germ, an acceptance of the phenomenon of death itself as it will confront him personally, body and soul. In his poor human fashion we may say that he wills to die with a "last intention."

It is at least conceivable that death is as profound an experience for the free Christian soul as for the body This experience, which lays bare the corporal-vital nature of the body in an unparalleled fashion, exposing the very roots of the composite nature of man, certainly is of supreme importance for the soul. All ascetical and pastoral literature demonstrates the point to satiety. We are unceasingly urged to "prepare" for death. And yet death is an act so strictly personal, so impervious to anticipatory experience, that it retains always for the investigator, for him who would prepare it, an unforeseeable, a unique character. Those who have experienced it are not in the habit of returning to us to elaborate its theoretical basis, and in such a situation we cannot but have recourse to a philosopher or a religious vision of the world.

Thomistic philosophy makes possible at least an approach to an understanding from without, of this phenomenon of death. From it we learn the possibility of corruption of the body and the necessity of the soul's enduring life. The soul, as the form of the body, cannot but be affected by the death of the body. Its function, during the period of the body's life, was to give to the body that life which is unremittingly exposed to death and finally dedicated to death. The ultimate situation of the body seems, in this philosophy, to be the dissolution with which it was threatened from the beginning. And, apparently, the soul, as the form of the body, would die as form at the same moment—whatever its future as separated soul.

But the soul is not only form, it is also subsistent; and as human, it is free. The situation in which it finds itself at the moment of death is far more decisive for itself than for the body, since the value of the soul is so far superior to that of the body. The soul's last moment on earth cannot but have for it a tragically weighty significance, and in its supreme agony we would expect it to be supported by its own liberty and upheld by the aid of the body. The act that closes human life would thus be human in the fullest sense of the word: an act prepared by human liberty throughout its length, inserted in the context of human history, freighted with the individual history of this soul, and stamping with a human consistency, for eternity, the human character of the soul.[4]

In an act of such decision it appears possible that the personal freedom of the composite person could be engaged to an extent hitherto unrealized. Disengaging itself from the body, the soul freely assumes a consistent attitude to the world of values which was not realizable to this extent in its temporal life. At the moment when the human personality is reflected with the least clarity in the expressions of the body, it assumes its greatest clarity as freedom, unifying the past and totalizing its experience in a choice that expresses itself finally.

It would, indeed, be difficult in a sane conception of death to conceive of this great recapitulation of life as wholly deprived of a free response. The stages of freedom, laden with imposed influences—social, religious, family, biological—which the soul has known in its life of union with the body, have been stages of a freedom gradually determining itself and liberating itself from all determinisms. The life that the soul is to lead in its future existence is marked by a free adherence to the supreme good, or a free aversion from it. That the decisive moment of death should fail in freedom would seem to imply that human death was assimilated only to animal death, was removed from conscious prolongation of Christ's activity on the Cross.

The whole of life having been a preparation for the attitude that the soul takes up at this moment, it would appear meaningless that this attitude should not be chosen lucidly and deliberately. The inconsistencies that marked the moral acts and even the moral attitudes of the man should be submissive here to a supreme choice that expresses and sums up his choices.

The fact that he is a being operating in time, choosing with a liberty relative to change, has been at once the risk and the salvation of man. Such choices could with difficulty determine within their own series the total moral being of the man who makes them, since they can be changed as long as the man continues to exist in time. They can be and doubtless are decisive for his eternal salvation, but at the same time they leave certain doors open, certain areas of his personality incompletely engaged.

The act which is to complete and summarize the human series of moral acts would seem to be itself a moral act that realizes the possibilities of good or evil, not merely at the level of motivation or act, but at the level of being itself. Death would thus involve a choice which sums up all previous choices in one, because it expresses the underlying orientation of the soul in a fully conscious manner. The partial and fluctuating determinations of oneself that had preceded this ultimate choice would naturally retain their full moral and religious importance, preforming the final liberty without necessitating it. Personal moral autonomy, acquired painfully and at varying levels during life, would at the last moment of life assume a completeness for good or for woe that would mean the final fulfillment of man as free.

The human development has thus far taken place with the body as its substratum. At death, when separation from this unfree foundation for freedom takes place, it would seem that spiritual maturity becomes possible in a new sense. At the moment of conscious death, all previous values are re-evaluated and the soul chooses its attitude before its Creator with awareness of the commitment it makes. The previous choices are seen as preparations that do not completely sound the possibilities of the concrete personality but rather prepare for its total expression at death. The assumption of this irrevocable attitude could hardly be other than the expression of those lesser choices which had educated the personal liberty.

Occasionally, these "final option" theories have been so proposed as to seem to reduce the significance of the human choice of this life. These are left with a minimal importance while a final option made at or even after death secures for man the mature expression of his personality. But it is evident that a choice made after death is in no wise consonant with Christ's emphasis upon this life's choices.

It should also be clear from the Gospels that the decisive importance of the choices made all during this life cannot be wiped out by the final attitude that the soul assumes before death. On the contrary, if such a final choice exists, it is undoubtedly the *expression* of the man such as he has formed himself by previous choices, although these choices may have lain at a deeper level of his personality than is immediately clear to him. The choice, if it is to be an expression of the person, cannot be discontinuous with the person's past. Its very purpose is to express that past with a completeness and a depth that has not been possible in choices more intimately affected by time.

What such a choice excludes is rather the puerile concept of final perseverance which seems to present God as engaged in a whimsical game in which he calls the soul to enter eternity through a passage beset with ambushes. In the great Christian perspectives the perils of the soul at death are by no means unrelated to the pattern of the moral life. The moral life of man is integral; otherwise states of grace and of sin could alternate in a meaningless fluctuation. More than any other sphere of man's activity, the moral life constructs human personality. It is absurd to think that the decisions we have made in the past do not weigh upon present and future choices. Our past inscribes itself upon our spirit as well as upon our body. Nor would the final option allow hardened sinners an easy last-moment conversion. It would be a moral miracle were the soul so to revoke all that has constituted its spiritual past. The tragic risk is rather that such a hardened sinner will render his freedom consistent in adhering more fully to evil.

The self-construction that takes place in a soul choosing evil will be the more fearful because the more free. In this case hell is the term of the soul's development, and in hell its option will be ratified for eternity. Man is capable of turning his liberty in the direction of hell long before death. Acts that engage man's full liberty may be less frequent than is sometimes thought, but Christian tradition is very clear about the fact that man can place acts that merit hell long before the moment of death.

There is, however, another class of sinners whose soul is the scene of living contradictions, the battleground of Satan and the Spirit. There are those who love God freely, but not without a struggle, whose passing acts at times contradict their enduring attitudes, whose thirst for God is not appeased by creatures but who nevertheless remain torn between self and God until the final moment. For such as these death assumes a clarifying role.

There are also the saints whose efforts at the total gift, as they are so painfully aware, have been so incomplete, so much in need of repetition. For such as these death assumes the role of the final invitation. The liberty that they have arduously constructed for themselves by repeated choices now offers them the opportunity adequately to express themselves. The saint's option for God over self has been repeated so often that there is no likelihood that the last choice will be anything but the total act of love for which he has sought and prepared.

The witness at a death agony is no doubt tempted to consider death in its passive aspect rather than in the supreme dynamism described by modern theologians. But of course all one can see in the observable fact of death is its exterior, the progressive dissolution of the composite. And death, as Heidegger remarks, is always interior, personal. The theologian is not concerned with *appearances* of death but with the interior acts, which may or may not take place at that precise moment when the bodily preparations for dissolution are completed. To accept and affirm one's creaturely status at this moment, with all that the status of creature implies, remains at least a possibility.

It is true than neither Scripture nor Tradition, the

sources of revelation, give any confirmation of the theory of the final option which the theologians propose; it is wholly in the realm of theological speculation. Nevertheless such thought has genuine values; it represents an attempt to answer the questions raised by modern philosophy, and by theology itself, concerning the problem of death. If one can at best only call the answers suggested by such speculations possible, it remains true that possibilities have their theological importance.

The philosophers who have posed the question of the meaning of death might find in revelation many indications of a solution. The interiorization of death, its capacity to give deeper meaning to life, are not themes foreign to theological thinking. Revelation, like Christ Himself, is always contemporaneous to each succeeding age. Theologians are aware of the repeated calls of the Church to speak the message of Christ in terms that enlighten their contemporaries, since theology must progress and develop in living contact with all that is valid in contemporary thought, whatever its source. For this reason, many of the leading theologians of the day are seeking for a more complete elaboration of a theology of death.

However, a complete theology of death would have to offer some light on such questions as the relation of human to animal death, the relation of the "separated soul" to the material cosmos before the Resurrection, the relation of death as "natural" to death as "punishment" in the concrete order, the relation of death to personal grave sin, to the dominion of the devil, and many other questions.

But from what we have already considered the religious significance of Christian death begins to emerge. It is at once apparent that Christianity concerns itself with the salvation of the entire man, body and soul. It has no interest in man disembodied, or detached from his context in history. All the Church's thoughts and the whole of her love are bent upon man as God made him: body and soul.

So too the Christian doctrine of salvation is too realistic to be concerned about any kind of inhuman happiness for human beings. Christ is risen body and soul, and in Him we will rise; this is the central expression of the doctrine of the Church on death, a doctrine marked by a profound and courageous optimism. Christ is risen and in Him we are risen, body and soul, in hope. As St. Athanasius remarks, "Since the day when the Savior rose from the dead, death is no longer a fearful thing. All those who believe in Christ know that in dying they no longer perish and that the resurrection will render them incorruptible."

The authentic Christian attitude is thus always a waiting for the Parousia, the second coming, when the full glory of Christ's Mystical Body will shine forth in His members. Death for the Christian is essentially a joyous affair. Did not St. Cyprian protest at the gloom and mourning with which we surround death? We note too that in Christian spirituality death is essentially an affair of the whole community; it has an ecclesiological significance. The entire Church will rise, and at the Last Judgment the triumph of Christ will be visible to all in all His members.

The student of St. Paul in particular cannot but realize that death has been transformed by the death and resurrection of Christ. For now it is true to say that in the exact measure that death is accepted as the term of our human life, in that measure a man's thought is no longer Christian. For to St. Paul and to the early Christian death is not a decisive ending introduced suddenly into human life; it is rather the triumphant beginning of our new life in Christ.

Nor do we wait until the end of life to experience death. As we have seen, the Christian's first experience, precisely *as* a Christian, is the experience of death in Baptism: at once the introduction to the Christian life, a death and a resurrection. The Christian is plunged into the death and resurrection of Christ and emerges united to the living and glorious Christ who bears with Him always the effects of His death and resurrection. Indeed some theologians would have it that the sacramental symbol of Baptism actually renders the death and resurrection of Jesus present in a mysterious fashion to the baptized soul, permitting the Christian to commune with those trans-temporal events.

Again, death is no stranger to the Christian experience during the course of life. For if Baptism plunges the Christian into the death and resurrection of Christ, the whole of man's spiritual life renders this death operative, for man dies mystically daily; he dies to sin and rises to newness of life. When the moment comes for the Christian to take leave of this passing phase of his existence on earth, he is again introduced into the mysteries of Christ: now for all eternity everything in this experience of temporal death has been transformed in its meaning for the Christian.

The soul, following after and prolonging the mystery of Christ its Head, strengthened by the Eucharist, the bread of life, descends with Christ to death, tastes with Christ the final victory over death, over the Adversary and over the powers of hell. The Christian soul triumphs in the triumph of Christ, his Head.

Incorporated in a realistic fashion into Christ, the Christian dies in Christ. And his death is dominated by the drama which unrolled between Good Friday and Easter Sunday. For death is essentially a Paschal mystery. It is but the last, or the next to the last, step in the process of our conformation to Christ which began at Baptism. It may well be the last step, if the soul goes directly to heaven. It will be the next-to-last step if the soul's purification is continued in purgatory, where at the hands of the Divine Teacher it learns the demands of its own love, inadequate but piercing, for the uncreated love. The Christian death is the experience of a spiritual victory; it is a sharing with the victory of Christ, the eternal victim and victor.

In short, for the Christian, death interrupts nothing; it destroys nothing; it liberates, not from the body, but from the empire of sin. "Our Sister Death" is one more victorious stage in the development of the soul's freedom. One more stage, not yet the last, for even if received directly into heaven the soul still waits. It awaits the glorious resurrection of its body and of the whole glorious Church, the Bride without spot or blemish. It awaits the Last Judgment, the definitive victory of the whole Christ.

# 4

# JUDGMENT

As soon as it has left this temporal existence the soul is brought under the judgment of God. The light of eternity falls upon it with a clarity that enables the soul to perceive its own moral state and the past and future contained therein. Separated as it is from the body, which was once the instrument of its knowledge, the soul no longer knows in the labored, piecemeal fashion of its earth-bound days, but with an interior lucidity—direct, immediate, experiential—poured into its intelligence by Sovereign Truth. In the depths of this quickened consciousness there is now diffused an illumination that judges all its history. The corridors of the past are flooded with light and the accomplishments of a lifetime yield themselves at once and without pretense or subterfuge to the evaluation of a mind beyond the hazard of self-deceit. Through the impact of divine power the soul sees with inevitable clarity all of its omissions and achievements, its words and deeds and motives.

It is the Divine Judge who impresses upon the awakened soul both the sentence of eternity and the understanding of that sentence in one act of power and enlightenment. His glance reveals to the soul its future, together with all its conditions and causes. And the created intelligence ratifies this equitable decision, for it grasps the significance of the case. The word of the Sovereign Judge evokes this immediate judgment in a soul brought for the first time to a truly total view of the reality of itself and its personal history.

Thereupon it fulfills this sentence in a comprehending spirit and passes to heaven, hell, or purgatory, there to await the General Judgment, the final triumph of Christ, the revelation of the mysteries of existence and history and the judgment of the world.

Of the Last Things the one on which primitive Christianity most insists is the dogma of the General Judgment. Christ affirms many times in the Synoptic Gospels that it is He, in His character as Man, who will judge humanity and the human historical process. St. Matthew has evoked this scene for us in detail: "When the Son of Man comes in his glory, and all the angels with him, he will sit down upon the throne of his glory, and all nations will be gathered in his presence, where he will divide men one from the other, as the shepherd divides the sheep from the goats; he will set the sheep on his right, and the goats on his left.

"Then the King will say to those who are on his right

hand, Come, you that have received a blessing from my Father, take possession of the kingdom which has been prepared for you since the foundation of the world. For I was hungry, and you gave me food, thirsty, and you gave me drink; I was a stranger, and you brought me home, naked, and you clothed me, sick, and you cared for me, a prisoner, and you came to me. Whereupon the just will answer, Lord, when was it that we saw thee hungry, and fed thee, or thirsty, and gave thee drink? When was it that we saw thee a stranger, and brought thee home, or naked, and clothed thee? When was it that we saw thee sick or in prison and came to thee? And the King will answer them, Believe me, when you did it to one of the least of my brethren here, you did it to me.

"Then he will say to those who are on his left hand, in their turn, Go far from me, you that are accursed, into that eternal fire which has been prepared for the devil and his angels. For I was hungry, and you never gave me food, I was thirsty, and you never gave me drink; I was a stranger, and you did not bring me home, I was naked, and you did not clothe me, I was sick and in prison, and you did not care for me. Whereupon they, in their turn, will answer, Lord, when was it that we saw thee hungry, or thirsty, or a stranger, or naked, or sick, or in prison, and did not minister to thee? And he will answer them, Believe me, when you refused it to one of the least of my brethren here, you refused it to me. And these shall pass on to eternal punishment, and the just to eternal life." (Matt. xxv, 31-46.)

St. Paul, in the Second Epistle to the Thessalonians (i, 9-10), describes the triumph of Christ: "The presence of the Lord, and the majesty of his power, will condemn them to eternal punishment, when he comes to show how glorious he is in his saints, how marvelously he has dealt with all the faithful."

And again in Romans (ii, 16): "And there will be a day when God (according to the gospel I preach) will pass judgment, through Jesus Christ, on the hidden thoughts of men."

Christ will come to judge this world, this scene of His sufferings and humiliations, and He will come as Victor and Illuminator. Then will He be definitely revealed as King of a universe now entirely submissive to His regal power. Then will He unveil the mysteries of His providence over the world. The effects of all human actions upon the destiny of this cosmos will be made clear, and justice will triumph with a triumph which is absolute. During the course of temporal existence it was impossible to pass a final judgment upon the ensemble of created reality or upon the individual acts which inserted themselves into the context of history. Now Christ will be manifested as the living center of humanity, whose whole significance flows from Him. He will exercise His judicial power to glorify His Church and to proclaim the existence of sovereign goodness operative in the redemption of the world. The record of every individual with all its actions and motives will be reviewed and receive its reward or punishment. All existence, all that was done in time, will be submitted to this clarifying light of judgment.

This judgment, moreover, will disclose the vast plan for the redemption of humanity and the roles played by individuals and groups as this plan worked itself out. The confusions and obscurity of history will be dissolved as all things are seen in relation to that divine Word in whom they were made.

Beyond all else, it is the triumphant proof of God's redemptive love that will then emerge. For the judgment is ordained to manifest not the punitive powers of God but His all-conquering goodness. It will be discovered then by everyone how truly Jesus is to be defined in terms of love and how fitting it is for men to be appraised in terms of their relationship to Jesus. The position which a man took up on earth towards the Savior and His atonement will be decisive here. Sin will be unmasked and shown as the suicidal madness it is. The sinner who refused the advances of Christ will see absurdity streaming through the whole range of his being. The self-hatred which was the wellspring of the rejection which sin implies will be disclosed.

Any effort to interpret God's will expressed in the moral law as a frustrating burden upon man is annihilated now in the blinding vision of salvific love. All the demands of God upon man will be set forth in their true nature, as an espousal of the interests of man. The commandments of God will put off their exterior aspects of imposed authority and reveal their inner nature as the laws according to which man's being expands. They will be grasped even by the sinner as exteriorizations of an inner attitude of love on God's part. The dynamism of Christian life will yield up its secret to examination and will be revealed as love. "At evening we shall be judged by Love," and Love will judge our deeds and character, omissions and motives.

In the light of eternity the Christian vocation will be understood as what it is: a vocation to love which effects the growth of man to maturity. Law and love will be seen in their original unity. The revelation of God concerning Himself will be seized in its full implications, and the liberty of the children of God will be made manifest.

The Christian, moreover, has lived in the close unity of the body of the Church, supported by the efforts of others, and himself giving impetus to the life of the whole. All the activities of the individual Christian have had their effects upon the whole body, and this inter-reaction of individual upon individual and upon the Church will be revealed to the society of the faithful in all its social import. A collective illumination will aid the faithful to judge the universal moral order, and there will be no more room for the questioning of history; it will have yielded up its innermost secrets, and all the intertwining series of causes and effects will be laid bare. The labors of the saints will be seen in their full depth and extent, which exceed the dimensions of their particular historical period. The collaboration of man with the labor of the eternal Father and Christ will be unmistakable. It will be the triumph of a society: the Church.

As the Christian has begun his life as a member of a society and has fostered that life within a society, so his final judgment will be social. The consummation of all things within the unity of the Mystical Body of Christ being now completed, the Christian will pass to the social life of the new Jerusalem.

# 5

# REDEMPTIVE
# SUFFERING

    Christian tradition is unanimous in affirming that the soul after death and before its reception into heaven is in a state of cleansing suffering. The ordinary man who steps from the sphere of temporal life into the sphere of the eternal, into the presence of the all-holy God, surely discovers within himself certain deficiencies which bar him from the total enjoyment of heaven. He must be purified, he must be prepared, he must be changed if he is to dwell in the presence of the all-holy God. And in some mysterious fashion, suffering enters into this purgation. This is the Christian faith. And yet the origins of this belief in purgatory are shrouded in obscurity.

## SUFFERING IN THE OLD TESTAMENT

If we turn to the Old Testament we find that it offers little interpretation of suffering either in this life or in the next. The early Hebrews did not even pose the problem of suffering and of evil in a theoretical way. They knew certainly that evil is a daily experience and that much of man's activity is spent in trying to avoid suffering. They felt the same pressures that the world knows today: famine, war, sickness, death and poverty. But the problem of pain was seen by the Israelites from the special viewpoint of their faith: they never considered suffering or evil an occurrence due to the caprice or anger of demons or superhuman beings whom they had to placate. Magic and taboo had no role in Jewish religion.

Nor was Israel ever tempted to regard suffering as an illusion that man could correct by turning his mind in another direction. Neither did the pious Jew expect that the day would come when his control over the forces of nature would be such that he could obviate all distress. God was far too close in all the mysterious forces of nature itself for such a concept to enter the Israelite mind. For Israel, God was the master of life and of all its situations, painful or not.

The strong sense of community that dominated Jewish consciousness explains in part the relative indifference with which the suffering of the individual seems to be regarded in the Old Testament. Not that pictures of profound individual grief are absent from Old Testament literature. One has only to think of the parting of Naomi and Ruth, of Anna's tears over her childlessness and David's over Absalom.

But the sorrow of individuals is portrayed in very dispassionate fashion. The great theme is the continuity of this chosen people. For the sake of the community it may be necessary at times that the individual suffer. Abraham had to abandon his home and fatherland and offer Isaac to God, but in the end he is the father of a great people. Moses suffers from the opposition and distrust of his people, but he leads them out of Egypt. Elias, Amos, Micheas are experienced in suffering, but they fulfill their tasks as prophets. Osee suffers deeply from his wife's wayward conduct, but through her he learns by contrast the tenderness and fidelity of God's love for Israel. The nation comes to know the humiliation of the exile, but the power and wisdom of God are made manifest through their trials.

Not only does the individual come closer to God through his misfortunes, but he aids his own people by bearing patiently the scourges God sends to him. Jacob draws spiritual profit from the loss of his child, and his family grows into a great nation. Joseph is hated and feared by his brothers; but he is destined to become their salvation in time of distress. Daniel is persecuted, but Babylon's king is converted to the service of Yahweh. God's plans for salvation may be unfathomable, but at times at least a glimpse of the meaningfulness of suffering is granted.

The close alignment between sin and suffering is repeatedly stressed by the Old Testament. Fear of suffering tempts man to disobey Yahweh and leads him on many an occasion to abandon God and commit sin. This choice, multiplied throughout the whole kingdom, affects the course of the history of Israel and brings down God's punishment. War and famine, poverty and sterile idleness are God's judgment upon a rebellious people. After these tribulations Israel frequently repents, prays for pardon and receives salvation from Yahweh.

Thus history moves in the cycles of spiritual crisis. The sufferings of Israel are all part of a great drama illuminating this single theme: the Almighty is just and will not tolerate unrighteousness. Each new generation adds its own variations to the story, but the theme is one: there is a great conflict in the world between the God of Israel, who will not endure evil, and the pride and sinfulness of man. Suffering is but the logical consequence of this conflict. Because God retains His almighty power and because man continues to sin, each succeeding generation witnesses the consequence of sin in its own suffering.

The great prophets of Israel were not philosophers, but they had their own explanation of the suffering they saw about them. What we recognize in them above all else is their completely single-hearted devotion to the Faith of Israel. They knew that evil is man's act of rebellion against the will of the Lord, and they knew that as a result of this moral evil God sends suffering as a judgment. The idea that the innocent within the community might also be hurt does not seem to perturb them. Perhaps they realized that there were none who could be called completely innocent. But they strike out vigorously and in torrential language against the man who freely enters the camp of evil and thus becomes the deliberate cause of individual and social suffering.

In Isaias, the redemptive character of suffering is luminously revealed by the figure of the tragic "Servant of

God," whose punishment and pain wins the entire world to the cause of justice. This Servant of God is a mysterious figure, but there is no doubt that the author intends him as a man who suffers with a mission—the redemption of the world.

In Jeremias, one of the most tempestuous of the prophets, we notice for the first time the expressions of impatience with God because of personal griefs. Jeremias later anticipates the attitude of Job when he reproaches God for sending him these endless troubles. He wonders whether it would not have been better to remain unborn rather than to endure such sufferings and vexations.

Yet even Jeremias does not attempt to give us a philosophy of suffering. He is too concerned with lodging his complaint against God for His bitter treatment of him. He does ask for the first time why God keeps silent while the wicked prosper and the just suffer. He wonders whether God will tolerate the situation always, and he asks what justice there is in permitting the wicked to win victory after victory over the just people. The answer is simply that God is just and has all things in His power; no matter how things appear to be now, in the end the just man will triumph because God remains at his side.

The psalms are full of the details of personal sufferings. We read of sickness and death, of physical distress, mental anguish and torture. Many of these, moreover, are visited upon God's friends. Despite this fact, the psalms consistently repeat the same theme to Israel: the just man is victorious. It is true that his victory is not always observable or validated by evidence, but the preservation of faith is in itself the great conquest. The wicked seem to prosper and enjoy the good things of this life, but the answer to the psalmist's puzzled questioning is always a total faith in the God of Israel.

There is, however, a suggestion that the prosperity of the wicked is not enduring, because their death will take it away. Just and unjust go down to death, but the psalms speak of the death of the just in a way that distinguishes it sharply from the death of the unjust. Death is never absent for the unjust man. It hangs over him constantly as the threat of Yahweh. And when it does come, it comes in dreadful form, either prematurely, or through a terrible sickness, or accompanied by the unhappiness of ill health, lack of prosperity and misfortune in his family. No matter how secure the wicked may seem, they are setting the stage for a terrible last act: the vengeance of God.

The Wisdom literature, with the exception of Ecclesiastes, maintains the same characteristic universal outlook. Proverbs insists over and over again that God distributes justice to the holy and the sinner alike. He rewards them according to their deeds because He himself is just and powerful. Those who seek Him always prosper, those who are charitable, temperate, prudent and wise will arouse the envy of their neighbors in the end. Despite appearances the evil man is doomed beforehand; his lamp will be put out, his light will end and justice will be vindicated.

But we find a different strain in Ecclesiastes. This writer shows a form of cynicism which almost approaches Epicureanism. While he does not deny the existence of the righteousness of God, he declares that it is useless to attempt to know the secret of God's justice in dealing with this world. The problem of suffering is a vast and impenetrable mystery, and it is not profitable to spend much time exploring it.

Probably the most profound investigation of the problem of suffering appears in the book of Job. Satan has entered into a contest with God to debate the integrity of the goodness of Job. Job suffers all sorts of indignities; he loses his wealth, his possessions, his children, the love of his wife, the esteem of the community. And inevitably he asks: "Why do good men suffer?"

This is the climax of the second theme in Old Testament literature on suffering: the suggestion that in this world it is by no means evident how God rewards the just. Job's three friends give him the classic answers of Israel: God is an impartial, just judge and possibly Job is not guiltless himself. Job, who knows his own history, protests that he is innocent. He feels frustrated because he cannot persuade God to manifest this innocence before the world. As his persecution continues Job searches desperately and in every direction for a solution to the problem. For a moment he is consoled with the thought that perhaps when he is in his grave he will be permitted a vision of God standing at his side and vindicating him. As his anguish smolders he waves aside the solutions previously offered, his test assumes the proportions of an agony and he is drawn to the very brink of rebellion.

At the end, however, God comes to Job and annihilates his resistance. The Lord demands to know whether Job was present at creation. What indeed does Job know even of the natural mysteries which surround him—the lightning, the seas, the earth, the snow, the hail, the stars? In the presence of the great God of Israel Job recognizes his nothingness, his lowliness, his ignorance. When the superiority of Yahweh has been established the poet gives us one answer to the mystery of evil; simply a reaffirmation of the almighty power of the justice of God. Beyond this, reason must submit and man commit himself to faith in God.

What is most interesting about this book is Job's obscure idea that some vindication might come to him after the present life. He does not develop this theme, but there is a suggestion that he might be fully reconciled with God's judgment after his calamities on this earth have ended. And, at that point, the faith of Israel pauses; there is no full development of the theme of a justice awaiting eternity for its full vindication.

The beautiful text in the book of Machabees also testifies to the faith of later Israel in the vindication of the just and the final resurrection of the body. The sufferings that the seven brothers will endure on this earth will be recompensed by God later. Again, after the battle in which certain Jews have died after committing idolatry, Judas Machabeus causes a great collection to be made for the purpose of an expiatory sacrifice. It is evident that for Judas and the author of the book this sacrifice would be of assistance to the dead by purifying their souls at the moment of the Messianic resurrection.

But there is no clear suggestion in either of these two texts of the second book of Machabees that sacrifice will be of avail to the dead *immediately* after their entrance into eternity. There is no clear proof of what the Christian would call purgatory in these texts, though later tradition will indeed interpret them as a foundation for this belief. It is also noticeable that when one studies the biblical tradition concerning funerals one never reads of any prayers or sacrifices offered, as the Christian would say, for "the repose of the soul" of the dead.

## THE FAITH OF THE CHURCH

Whatever obscurity with regard to purgatory we find in Scripture, the attitude of the infant Church was perfectly clear. From the beginning Christians prayed for their deceased.[1] Since paganism had so many theories concerning the fate of the dead, the early Christians were profoundly concerned to know what they should believe in this regard. Certainly Our Lord had spoken frequently about eternal life. At the same time He and the Apostles had stated clearly that one enters into heaven only if one is sinless. When we remember that the young Christian community was made up of convert Jews and pagans it is very easy to understand the solicitous interest which it had in this question, for both pagans and Jews had their own ways of remembering the dead, their own cults and ceremonies and prayers. For centuries the pagans had guarded cults of the dead and solemnly observed, with libations and repasts at the tombs, the feasts of the dead.

Moreover, the Church's penitential discipline encouraged speculation concerning the fate of the dead. While she directed the faithful to pray daily for the forgiveness of their venial sins, she excluded from communion those who had committed grave sins. At times she imposed lengthy canonical penances. This raised an inevitable question: if a man died before fulfilling the whole of his penance, or if he had fulfilled none at all, what would become of his soul? Suppose a person fell dangerously ill, was given the sacrament and died immediately, before he had time for penance?

Naturally there were many misgivings on the part of Christians with regard to the complete sinlessness of their beloved dead, for not everyone was an Apostle or martyr. In the early Church, apparently, people thought that there were two different categories in eternity, the first composed of those who were with Christ in paradise —the Apostles, the martyrs, the Prophets—the second made up of ordinary Christians, for whom the Church prayed. The names of the dead were inscribed frequently on special lists read out during liturgical services. Mass was not offered for any particular soul, as is done today, but a general prayer was made for all the dead.

At certain times the early Christians also held solemn services at the burial places of the dead. In such surroundings they doubtless speculated upon the fate of their beloved friends and family. At times the Christians celebrated the Eucharistic sacrifice in cemeteries, and they accompanied this sacrifice by the offering of gifts and also by community feasts. The early Church was fully aware that there were many who had passed into the next world burdened with the heavy load of daily venial sins, and for these she prayed during the Eucharist. She did not seem to be entirely clear as to *where* these souls were or *how* prayers would help them, but she knew definitely that prayer and sacrifice could be of avail for these faithful Christians.

In the first period of Christian literature we do not find the expression *purgatory* at all, but we do meet frequent references to the "resting place" or "storerooms" of the dead. Quite early the Church underwent a development in regard to her prayers for the dead. In the beginning she had prayed for all her departed during Mass, but about the year 200 she began offering the Eucharistic sacrifice itself for her dead on their tombs the day of their burial. Later, private Masses were offered for individual souls. Before the seventh century we find the beginnings of confraternities whose object is to pray and fast especially for the departed.

We must note also that it was not only the Latins who had the habit of praying for the dead. St. John Chrysostom tells us that the custom dates back to Apostolic times. The Greek Church from the beginning joined in beseeching the Lord to grant "refreshment" to those who had fallen asleep in Him. St. Cyril of Jerusalem in his instructions to the people also treats of prayers for the dead and explains that prayer will be of benefit to them.

This ancient care to cherish the dead is a proof of the Church's universal belief in the existence of some intermediary state between heaven and hell. The liturgy of the first centuries also testifies to a belief in some form of purgatory. By the time of the Middle Ages the Roman liturgy had a beautiful formula for those who had gone ahead in the name of Christ: "Be mindful, O Lord, of Thy servants and handmaids . . . who are gone before us with the sign of faith and sleep the sleep of peace. To them, O Lord, and to all that rest in Christ, we beseech Thee, grant a place of refreshment, light, and peace through the same Christ Our Lord."

We may note, too, that many of the funeral descriptions of the primitive Christian Church bear evidence of its belief in the existence of purgatory. The Christians had taken over the pagan custom of inscribing a last wish for the dead on their funeral monuments. In the catacombs we see tombstones covered with inscriptions which express the Christian hope in an eternal life. Generally speaking, they echo the prayers of ancient liturgies. All these inscriptions bear eloquent testimony to the faith of the primitive Church in purgatory, because they testify to the belief that not all the dead are yet with Christ; by prayer and almsgiving the living can hasten their admission into the eternal light.

It is true that these inscriptions do not paint the state of the dead in very vivid colors; they are not particularly imaginative, and are, indeed, reticent. But they are witness to a belief in an intermediary state for the souls of the departed. From the third century on we hear also of the "cleansing" of the soul; consequently, the word "purgatory," which comes from that root, will seem a natural term for the condition or abode of the souls who have departed this life in union with Christ but burdened with a multitude of the smaller sins.

What we notice especially in the primitive Church is that its belief in purgatory was constantly developing. In fact it was rather a living practice than a speculative, doctrine, still less a well-developed systematic doctrine.

A certain vagueness concerning the state of the soul after death and before the Last Judgment continued well into the Middle Ages. In fact, in the fourteenth century Pope Benedict XII considered it wise solemnly to define that the souls of the saints attained to the vision of God as soon as they departed this life. He gave so detailed a definition concerning the state of the soul after death because the fairly common notion seemed to prevail that there were two paradises into which the happy soul might enter, a lower one somewhere on this earth, and an upper one in the celestial region. In the earthly paradise the souls prepared themselves to enter into the heavenly paradise. It was believed that the martyrs and the Prophets entered immediately into the heavenly paradise to be united with Christ, but that the other souls tarried in the lower paradise. But Benedict's formal teaching ended this temporary and interesting aberration.

While the thought of the final judgment was still the dominating perspective of the early Christian, these teachers are certain, however, that the souls of the dead do not merely sleep until Judgment Day. They enjoy refreshment, light and peace, or they undergo appropriate penalties according to their moral situation at death. It was believed, as we have seen, that apart from the martyrs and conspicuous saints, most Christians would have to undergo a process of purification in some mysterious abode, for man's works are imperfect and nothing imperfect can enter into heaven. The essential primitive belief is clear, and abides: the souls of the dead must be cleansed. It is only the mode of this process which remains vague. About it we know only that its accomplishment will be painful, and that the prayers and sacrifices of the faithful on earth will help the souls in purgatory.

It is evident once again that the Church has reflected deeply upon the contents of her own consciousness in proclaiming the doctrine of purgatory. She has lived by the principle which furnished the proof of the existence of purgatory, and it is her own tradition that she proclaimed in enunciating this doctrine.

This is not to say that one does not find in Sacred Scripture a point of departure for the proofs of the exist-

ence of purgatory. It is doubtless true that Scripture is
of aid here, but at the same time one must admit certain
deficiencies in some of the so-called classical proofs. The
most general proof arises from the fact that in both the
Old and the New Testament revealed doctrine strongly
emphasizes two complementary notions: personal responsibility for sin and the divine justice. The sinner is expected, even after pardon, to expiate his faults: he is
expected to apply to himself the fruits of Christ's redemption. Other texts suggest also the existence of some sort of
intermediary state after death. Evidently the text of the
second book of Machabees, xii, 39-46, while it does not
directly prove the existence of such an intermediary state,
represents the usefulness of prayers for those who have
passed to God with faults upon their souls.

But the great proof is drawn from the fullness of the
Church's self-consciousness; from the very beginning, as
we have seen, she prayed for the souls of her faithful departed, offered the Holy Sacrifice on their behalf. From
her constant solicitude for certain of her departed, it was
evident that her care for them had not ceased; that she
could not grow forgetful as long as any of her children
had not attained the rest of the Lord. But as she is compassionate, so she is discreet; it is not within the intention
of the Savior to reveal with any detail the nature of the
trial which must be undergone by the departed who are
not fully purified.

It is curious to note how the idea of a purifying fire
came to be connected with the Catholic belief in purgatory. In the oriental Church of the third century, Origen
wrote of a fire which cleansed the souls of those who had
passed to Christ. But the fire itself he identified with the

purifying fires of the Last Judgment. It was the day of judgment, and its supreme test, which would cleanse the vestigial imperfections of souls. In such a view of things, it is undeniable that the idea of purgatory, still awaiting full explication, was implicit, but from a somewhat obscure perspective. And this uncertainty is in turn joined to the early Christian belief that the souls, whether of just or damned, did not receive their final dwelling until after the Last Judgment. St. Paul, in his first letter to the Corinthians (iii, 13), illustrates the early Christian catechesis: the fire of the last day will purify the works of the imperfect.

This is the first form that Catholic belief took of purgatory—this fire of judgment. Many of the early Doctors of the Church expressed their belief in this fire of judgment and at times they extend this judicial fire to a description of purgatory. Certainly this is the case with St. Gregory the Great, who was to become the patron of all those authors who maintained that Christian purgatory is principally a suffering from fire. So, following the tradition, St. Cyprian, St. Augustine and Tertullian all mention certain purifying sufferings that the soul is subject to after death.

There are, then, admittedly a great number of patristic and liturgical sources which speak of "fire" in this connection, but there is no doctrine obliging the Christian to maintain that the souls in purgatory are tortured by fire. Whether the fire of the liturgical text is metaphorical or real, whether its primary reference is to the judicial flame of the Last Judgment rather than to purgatory, are other questions.

Nor is it revealed that purgatory, properly speaking, is

a *place;* it is true that we tend to think spatially because of our human experience, but when one is dealing with the situation of souls without bodies, spiritual terms are required. Purgatory is not so much a place as a situation or a state of soul. One could also criticize the divisions of time applied to purgatory in popular preaching, the years, days, months, of purgatory that must be fulfilled. It should be evident that the duration of souls does not obey the same law as the duration of bodies.

Popular preaching has also done a great disservice at times to the notion of purgatory by presenting it as a vast torture chamber where God exercises His "vengeance" upon the souls imprisoned there. The medieval mind, avid as it was of mystical visions and particularly preoccupied with the state of the dead, was over-rich in "revelations" concerning purgatory. These detailed descriptions, which create horror in the modern mind, are not to be taken as Christian doctrine.

## PURIFICATION AND GROWTH

The work of God goes on after death in purifying the souls attached to Him. Conscious that they have attained a state where they can no longer offend God and where the eternal vision of His face is assured to them, the souls in purgatory must know a deep interior joy. And yet they go through some process of development, of interior purification. Perhaps the suffering of the mystic most closely resembles the suffering of purgatory itself. One would

prefer to insist more upon the interiority of these sufferings
and less upon the notion of torture imposed from without.
Doubtless there is a penal and an expiatory element in
the sufferings of purgatory, but the most profound notion
of this mystery would include a new development of the
soul's energies in the direction of the God whom, in death,
the soul chose eternally. Purification then would include,
as any positive notion of the term must require, a growth
in love, a growth in singleness of regard, a willingness
to suffer one's state, and, in bearing it for love, to amelio-
rate it.

The state of the soul in purgatory is that of one who
has not loved purely enough, whose love has been vitiated
to a degree by less worthy attractions. The soul will be
detained until its full condition is realized, the pain of its
condition accepted, the remedy for its condition sought.
And when this condition is realized, the soul at length
will be able to concentrate all its energies, with the help
of the God who awaits it, upon an act of love that in its
intensity, duration and object, will be heaven itself.

In this view the purifying sufferings of purgatory are
the flames of charity which consumes the obstacles to
itself. The soul adheres to God with the fixity of one who
has found that for which his heart thirsted. All that could
separate the soul from the object of its love is detested,
and all that leads to more perfect union is embraced with
joy. So great is the fire of love which possesses the soul
from the moment of its entrance into purgatory that at
that very instant every venial sin is remitted. The soul is
substantially fixed in love of God, and the only changes
possible are in the direction of a growth in this love until
it breaks forth into the eternally unalterable love which

belongs to the celestial city. Whatever pains there may be in purgatory spring from this consuming love, and increase it. The soul rejoices that God has His way with it.

Purgatory responds to an ultimate need of the religious soul which confronts the absolute purity of God. Whatever be the goodness of man as he approaches the presence of infinite Goodness, he cannot but realize his own deep unworthiness. The memory of all the evil he has done and the good he has left undone, or accomplished partially or half-heartedly, would inspire distrust and anxiety were he not assured of a continuation of Christian purification in the next life.

Purgatory stands before the Christian conscience as an indication that the saving will of the Lord extends to the uttermost depths of man's being. A crisis of growth is still necessary to make progress possible. Purgatory represents that gracious possibility for interior development; it means liberation, fulfillment, realization.

The transforming action of Christ's redeeming grace has been inhibited in this life by a multitude of obstacles, obscure dynamisms which owe their power to the half-willed collaboration of man's freedom. Into all that is good man has injected a small portion of the cramping selfishness which halts his spiritual growth, and he is tempted to despair of that holiness and liberty to which the children of God are called.

The new life of Baptism, far from penetrating the depths of man's conscious psychic life, all too often has been merely juxtaposed to his natural life with its struggles for security, power and pride. The roots of even good acts are often hidden in a confused mélange of motives. He is aware that the growth made possible by grace has

not been completed; he is still immature in Christ. Light
has not flooded the darkness in which the soul is held
by the lower impulses; he has sought the darkness in
unacknowledged, devious fashion. He is only half-grown
to the full stature of Christ, because he has refused to put
away the things of a child. His spirit clamors for a decisive
leap to maturity. And purgatory prepares this development within the soul.

Far from being a vast organization of exterior tortures,
purgatory is a process of liberation and fulfillment. The
soul returns to itself, gathers its energies and becomes for
the first time its wholly ideal self. Spirits are not cleansed
in the same fashion as is matter. It is true that our faults
must be consumed to their depths, the confusions and
inconsistencies of life must be repaired, the debts of temporal punishment must be paid. But for such a process
the soul has no need of executioners and torturers, of fiery
demons and pools of sulphur, of the atmosphere of hell.

Suffering certainly attends the soul in purgatory, but
suffering is absent from almost no period of truly human
growth. To cast off old attitudes and remake one's self is
a painful, at times an agonizing experience, even in the
present life. In the process of healing the sick soul the
psychiatrist knows the anguish caused by uprooting the
knotted resistances to healing that the illness throws up.
But such agony is neither meaningless nor foreign. It is
the very source of growth. The first halting steps to maturity must be taken or the soul, twisted back on itself, will
have to repair in agony the willful regressions. When the
child passes from childhood to adolescence, when the
adolescent passes into maturity, there is the same element
of abandonment and search, trial and rejection, effort,

struggle, choice and growth, almost never free from suffering.

The emergence of the divine idea of the self in purgatory, accompanied as it is by purifying, cleansing, liberating suffering, is a process that should not strike fear into the hearts of those who are concerned for their beloved dead. The individual whose love is deep and pure has the capacity to rejoice at every genuine growth that promotes the values of the beloved. As the soul tried in the flames of divine love frees itself from the constricting forces of egotism, it becomes its valid self.

Catherine of Genoa has insisted upon this joyous aspect of purgatory, affirming that it is not possible to discover a greater contentment than that of the soul in purgatory unless it be the happiness of the elect in heaven. This happiness of purgatory must grow constantly as the soul is increasingly penetrated by the presence of God, who removes successively all obstacles to union. The imperfect possession of God that results from the soul's imperfect state requires indeed a fiery penetration of the soul to be purified, but it causes at the same time a joyous development. All that marks this soul as unique and precious becomes more fully realized in the process. An intensification of the genuine personal resources and values of the individual takes place. The particular and inimitable beauty of this personality is raised to a higher pitch, is concentrated in a wholly new fashion through the action of God upon the soul. The joyous suffering that is involved in purgatory is hastened by the exigencies of the loving soul who knows that at long last it cleaves to the Living God, the object of its final and total love.

As we have said, the form of duration of purgatory is

doubtless different from that of the earth. It has been suggested that the human mind, in speaking of days and years, may be translating the sufferings of an extreme instant in the terms of earthly duration. The time of purgatory is a time measured by development within the soul possessed, without remorse or rebellion, in the security of God's love. The past is not present to the soul as a source of embitterment, nor the future as a source of anguish and doubt. No one doubts that God's overwhelming power could effect this cleansing in an instant; by His power the soul's love for Him could be raised instantaneously to such a pitch of ardor as would burn away all imperfections. This He effects in the case of the martyrs who lay down their lives in testimony to His fidelity, but in the case of those to whom the grace of martyrdom is not granted, the purifying process seems to take place in a mysterious duration. The divine leaven of grace is penetrating the mass of earthly resistances in a fashion that transcends time.

Faith has not become vision, but its light falls with an almost experiential brilliance upon the spiritual events that take place between the soul and the living God into whose hands it has committed itself. Jesus is again the Divine Master, and none can equal Him for suavity of teaching. In this school the blessed souls can make their own the sentiments of St. Paul: "I am sure that neither death, nor life, nor angels, nor principalities, nor powers, nor things present, nor things to come, nor might nor height, nor depth, nor any other creature, shall be able to separate us from the love of God, which is in Christ Jesus our Lord" (Rom. viii, 38-9). The spell of temporal modes of thought is broken.

The early centuries of Christianity passed judgment upon the fate of those who had gone to sleep in the Lord by their choice of decorations in the Christian cemeteries. They have passed into the hands of the Liberator, as Daniel from the lions' den, as Noah from the deluge, as the three from the fiery furnace, as Jonas from the great fish, as Lazarus from the tomb.

# 6

# HELL

It was inevitable that the development of Israel's religious consciousness should involve a parallel expansion of the notion of retribution. As we have seen, the earliest Old Testament descriptions of *sheol* were of a place in which the shadowy dead were plunged into loneliness, silence and a drab existence, without relation to their merits. The concept of *sheol*, however, developed progressively throughout the Old Testament era. At first it simply suggested that curious state in which a man would find himself incapable of intellectual and affective life, knowing nothing of communication, intelligence, or wisdom. The semi-conscious sleepers wandering here are without voice or speech. All are indiscriminately mingled in this abyss whose walls of darkness only God can measure, whose total obscurity no sun ever pierces. Here where night and silence converge is the home of the worm and of blight. In this grave, all inhabitants, good and bad alike, are reduced to a gray existence.

## ETERNAL PUNISHMENT IN THE OLD TESTAMENT

But such a doctrine must naturally stir anxious inquiry. If the justice of God always balanced the scales on earth, this earliest conception of *sheol* would not be so disquieting. It becomes inconceivable, however, once the point is made that, as a matter of fact, the good do not always prosper and the wicked sometimes do. The realization that justice is not fulfilled in time occasionally takes the shape of a question in the Old Testament, for the uncertain sanctions of this earth are clearly not sufficient to curb evildoers. As the Israelite grew in awareness of his individual responsibility he frequently saw that divine retribution on this earth is not always fulfilled. Sometimes, for instance, the miserable lot of a just man like Job seems quite unproportioned to his devout life.

The uneasiness provoked by searchings of this sort was assuaged once *sheol* ceased to be represented as an eternal prison in which all the inmates served equal sentences and was thought of rather as a place of passage, a temporary abode from which both just and sinner depart to a different type of life. Occasionally this confidence of the just in some life after death is found in early Jewish history, but it becomes clearer in the later years.

For the Prophets it is the community of Israel rather than the individual on whom justice will focus. But even though they think of the resurrection as the re-establishment of the Israelite nation, still this is itself an image of the individual's bodily restoration. We can say, for instance, that the notion of Israel's national rebirth, the end of the Babylonian captivity and the return to the holy land, prepared the Jewish soul for the idea of personal immortality. From this time on it is certain that some victory over death is granted: Yahweh will exert his power and the just man will leave *sheol.* God will once more gather together the dispersed members of Israel.

In Jeremias we find great stress laid upon the related theme of individual responsibility. From the crucible of pain Israel's holy ones draw the lessons taught by suffering and national disaster. They are now concerned less with the restoration of the nation than with fidelity to God. Daniel, as we have already seen, announces clearly a personal resurrection at the end of the world when *sheol* has yielded its prey to a judgment in which the individual's own merits will play a decisive role. All men will leave the shadows of *sheol* to be judged. The radical distinction between just and sinner will be recognized and the order of justice re-established as the sinners go down into everlasting shame and the just man is recalled to joyous life. For this just man *sheol* will be only a transitory state interposed between our present mortality and future immortality: but for sinners *sheol* will be only the gateway to grosser suffering.

The Old Testament is reserved on the precise nature of these penalties but the joys of the just are vividly envisioned. It does seem, however, that later Jewish thought conceives of *sheol* not as a prison but as a furnace, in which fire will be the instrument of God's anger. The Book of Wisdom speaks emphatically of the spiritual and psychological aspects of eternal punishment: those in *sheol* will be stricken with terror and fear, and tormented by the absence of God. For the devout Israelite this last is the supreme horror of *sheol*. He has been separated from his God, and in this place of darkness he can no longer celebrate the rights of God.

There are many somber descriptions of ancient *sheol*, but the two chief characteristics, apart from this separation from God, are the worm and the fire. The worm is doubtless a metaphor indicating the reproach of personal consciousness. The fire too has its metaphorical element and points to the intensity of suffering in the souls who have lost their God for eternity. Yahweh is defined as a devouring fire. He is a jealous God whose anger will consume the outcast like a flame, licking the inmost depths of *sheol*.

## ETERNAL PUNISHMENT IN THE NEW TESTAMENT

In the New Testament Our Lord calls the abode of the damned *Gehenna*. This expression occurs eleven times in the Synoptic Gospels, and it has an interesting history.

In the literal sense it designates a ravine running north-west-southwest of Jerusalem. This spot had an evil reputation among the Jews because it was the infamous sanctuary of Moloch where living human victims were sacrificed. In New Testament usage Gehenna stands for the place of eternal damnation, a chamber of horrors into which the renegade will be plunged after death. Christ threatens with this awful fate those who are deficient in fraternal charity or who betray their neighbors. So terrible is it that if one had to choose between temporal death or a life of sin he should choose the former in order to avoid eternal Gehenna. The inmates of this dungeon are incapable of escape or rebellion and their hopeless prison resounds, says St. Matthew, with weeping and the gnashing of teeth.

As heaven is a country of light and joy, so hell is a night of blackness, cursing and pain. That careless man who came to the wedding without a suitable garment was cast into this dreadful darkness out of the warmth and brilliance of the wedding hall. Indeed, this opposition between light and darkness mirrors the opposition between Christ, the light of the world, and Satan, the prince of darkness, ruler of the damned and of the fallen angels.

Where the Old Testament stressed the worm and fire the New Testament undoubtedly prefers the latter image and calls hell the Gehenna of fire. At the end of the world the angels will separate the good souls from those evil ones who will be cast into the undying flames. The Apocalypse speaks of hell as a pool of fire and sulphur. And in the parable of the vine and the branches Christ makes it clear that those who have separated themselves from Him will be gathered up and cast into the fire.

The fire of hell is described as inextinguishable and eternal. Its smoke, says St. John, will rise for century upon century: there will be no rest either by day or by night for those who have adored the beast and his image. Certain of the texts which speak of fire, however, are evidently metaphorical, and what is clearly conveyed by this image is the burning suffering which is endured in hell. This note of pain is clearly delineated; obviously the pain is extreme.

One must recall, however, that the Oriental generally conveys truth beneath a structure of imaginative language. Thus heavenly happiness is represented under the image of banquets and nuptial feasts and hell is pictured under the image of a prison, a sepulchre where one is tortured by darkness, worms and fire. The characteristic element of fire in the biblical images of hell suggests the torture men dread most. It cannot but be that there is a real and objective sense to this torture by fire, but it is difficult to establish in what sense the image should be interpreted.

We may note also in the New Testament how frequently Jesus answers questions about the punishment of the unrepentant sinner by applying the traditional Jewish and pagan words: Gehenna, "down there," "in the darkness," "below." The word Gehenna conveys also the idea of a refuse heap upon which are tossed all the useless, consumed, or corrupted things of life.

Jesus has, however, also used for hell the very suggestive word "outside." Many of His parables on hell make it clear that eternity effects a radical separation between the good and the bad. The people of God, united in one family upon earth, will always be the family of God, and the condemned sinner will always be outside the family. In the parable of the net and the fishes some of the bad fish were cast out as useless and left to rot. In the parable of the cockle the noxious weed was finally torn up, burned and thrown outside. In His final discourse on the night before He died, Our Lord spoke of the true vine and the branches; of the condemned sinner who is cast out, cut off from the living branch of the family of God, delivered up to be burned.

Hell thus appears as a state of separation from God, a state of eternal hopelessness and uselessness. One is cut off from the land of the living, from the human family, the family of God, and has entered into the kingdom of the dead. When Our Lord speaks of the Last Judgment, he quotes his own terrible words to the damned: "I know you not." Surely few human words have evoked so terrifying a situation so briefly; the sinner is branded as the eternal stranger to the Redeemer. All the knowledge that the Lord had of His own creation, all the encounters in the sacraments and at prayer between the soul of man and his Creator—all these are canceled. "I do not know you." The choice of darkness over light, of stranger over friend, of chaos over order, of separation over union—this has not been the decision of Christ. It is the sinner's own final choice in the most rigorous, irrevocable sense, and here, at judgment, it is ratified by the Savior who is also Judge.

Now there can be no doubt that Christ's words, harsh, unequivocal, and lucid, are a stumbling block to the non-Christian mind of today. How synthesize the tenderness and compassion of the Good Shepherd with the hard justice of these apocalyptic passages? The synthesis is a difficult one indeed; but modern thought has made it nearly impossible. Sentimentality, secular humanism, and determinism have produced their own bitter fruit: the defiling of the sense of the transcendent majesty of God, and of the inescapable responsibility of man's moral choices. It is no longer generally believed, to put the matter bluntly, that man is capable of choices that could bring him to eternal death. The center of gravity in human life has shifted imperceptibly from eternal-values to temporal ones, from intellectual values to emotional ones.

We have become man-centered in an unfortunate manner. For when the pre-established hierarchy of goods is deserted and a value distorted from its proper position, that value is not honored but defiled. This is perhaps what modern man has done to humanistic values. In an attempt to exalt man he has dehumanized him. He no longer believes himself capable of choices meriting an eternal death. He no longer has any deep sense of responsibility for personal choices and fails to recognize the inner importance of those personal attitudes taken towards God and one's neighbor.

If we shift our viewpoints from eternal values to temporal ones, from God to man, we cannot but suppose that hell is unthinkable. It goes counter to all our humanistic, humanitarian sentiments. The thought of an eternal punishment is not only inconceivable but even unbelievable. Our sympathies for our fellowmen are lively, and we cannot help but put ourselves in the place of God as their judge. We point out the loving aspects of Christ and of God, and we feel that there is a contradiction between what He has revealed about His love for us and this doctrine of eternal hell-fire.

## UNDERSTANDING HELL

But of course the truth remains. The dogma of hell is fundamental in the Christian religion, and in the history of the Church it has never been challenged. To grasp it, however, we need to have a somewhat more intelligent comprehension of ourselves and of God than is common today. In order to understand hell one must understand the significance of mortal sin, for if sin itself is mysterious, then its sanction is equally so. It will help first of all to dispense with the bric-a-brac with which this subject is so often adorned by pulpit oratory. To do so is not to criticize famous preachers of the past. They had a particular end in view: to bring home in concrete and emotional language the reality of hell. But their descriptions are not always to be taken literally. Some of them indeed seem to have had an entirely undue familiarity both with the topography of hell and the details of life there.

It is perhaps inevitable that the human mind thinks of hell in terms of mythical representations; we are too unfamiliar with God to realize that His loss makes hell. The art of Bosch and Breughel—which won for the latter the title of "Hell Breughel"—the luxuriantly detailed descriptions of Dante, are closer in their conceptions to the pagan ideas of hell than to the Christian world of revelation. The idea of an underworld cosmos ordered exclusively to torture the enemies of God reflects in a symbolic fashion the intuition of St. Ignatius Loyola of all creaturedom arrayed against the sinner, but these artistic representations can lead the mind astray. Imagination is not a trustworthy guide before this mystery of malice and of justice that is hell.

Hell is an utterly serious subject and should not be treated with exaggeration, lest the contemporary listener dispense with so essential a belief because his more developed sensibilities are offended by a comic-opera approach to this reality. Hell is a dogma which reveals both the meaning of man and the seriousness with which God wishes it to be taken. If we did not accept the doctrine of hell, we would not really understand the dimension of a personal liberty which implies that our personal decisions can put us there.

Hell has been called "the risk of God." We should not think of it as God's vengeance upon the unrepentant souls who desert Him, for hell is much more their creation than His. The man who dies in unrepented mortal sin damns himself. For hell does not issue from an arbitrary decision of God. It is the direct and logical prolongation of man's own will to sin. If a man fixes himself in opposition to God, then hell is only the logical working out of this everlasting opposition. Anthropomorphic conceptions picture a Creator resentful at the usurpation of His authority. This is a caricature which represents God as one whose authority can be thieved, whose position is precarious and who feels the insecurities and the resentments that a man with human authority experiences. The psychological genesis of such a portrait is perhaps a man's projection of his own enmity towards God directly upon the Creator, so that he comes to think of God as hostile to himself. But God wills for man only the full deployment and development of all human capacities for happiness. God is motivated only by love in His actions, and hell is only a proof of the totality and the greatness of God's love for man.

God made man for life. He made him with all his possibilities for development and expansion following upon creation, and God is constantly at work enlarging man's being. He has even poured forth on man a fourth grade of vital activity which we call grace. Christ describes His eternal Father as a husbandman, a farmer who labors lovingly at the work of developing man. It is the wish of the eternal Father that we co-operate with Him in unfolding our own inner possibilities. Time is lent to man for the continued flowering of his capabilities. It is the era of growth in which a personal life develops toward that heaven where eye hath not seen nor ear heard of, nor has it in fact entered into the mind of man, to conceive the joys God has laid up for him.

Yet Christian teaching makes it eminently clear that hell also exists, and the teaching here is based upon some of the clearest statements Scripture has given us on any data of revelation. Hell is repeatedly mentioned by the loving Christ even at that most intimate moment of His life, the Last Supper. In fact one notices a rather consistent development of the subject by Our Lord. It is not because He rejoices at the thought of this eternal punishment falling upon members of His flock, but because He knew what was in man and the risk which human freedom involves.

The idea that the sinner is eternally condemned to darkness, eternally separated from Christ, seems fundamental to the entire concept of hell as Our Lord develops

it. At death the unrepentant sinner will be immobilized
in a darkness that is an eternal separation from the light.
The soul in hell must suffer intolerable aimlessness: since
all our nature, all our actions are framed in finality. As
intelligent human beings we constantly pursue aims, and
the man who has no aim suffers on this earth even from
his own lack of direction. To be frustrated of our aims
causes us a partial dissatisfaction or anguish even in this
life. But when the soul arrives in hell with a clear vision
that God is its final end, that God is the good for which
its entire nature hungers, it must be filled with a stormy
longing for the absolute.

The great passion of man, whether he realizes it or not,
is for his own total good, God Himself. The whole nature
of man is magnetized by this total goodness of God, the
source and sum of all that has value. It is possible for a
man to conceal this from himself while he is living and
to ignore the fact to a certain extent. But in the clear light
that falls upon him when he steps from the sphere of
temporal history into eternity he can no longer help recog-
nizing the unchanging passion of his soul for good, for
God. At the same time the soul realizes that it has lost
its good and has lost its eternity. It is remarkable that
among all pre-Christian descriptions of the world of the
dead—and they are many—none but the Israelite evokes
this anguished sense of the loss of God.

Our whole being is a thirst for love. In hell there is no
affection, and yet the soul feels an intimate nostalgia for
love. Even in this life we often see a soul tortured at the
realization that one whom he or she loves does not return
that love. And yet to be rejected by a human being is not
comparable to rejection by the loving God who will not

admit the damned soul to His presence. On earth we can always console ourselves with the reflection that the other human being is fallible in his judgment and does not understand our true inner worth. But we cannot persuade ourselves of that in our relationship with God. The soul in hell realizes that God is not animated by aversion, nor is He partial or distorted in His judgment. The rejection that occurs here is not the rejection of one, equal by another. It is a rejection of man by his Creator; a rejection of the soul by the source and goal of its being; a rejection of the finite by the infinite. Such a realization of aimlessness and lovelessness penetrates much more deeply into the soul of the damned than could any human, fallible rejection.

As human beings we are destined for a community life. We are not atoms or closed monads. We require sympathy and love for our development and growth. As normal men we wish to express our sympathies and love and we wish a return of love, which of its very nature launches this appeal for reciprocity. Yet the soul in hell must be aware that he receives no sympathy from those others in this dread "community." Hell is not the domain of love. Dante wrote above its door "Abandon hope, all ye who enter here," but he might also have written "Abandon all hope of love, ye who enter here." The soul in hell is in an eternal vacuum of the emotions, violently existing in the face of one long thirst for love.

The psychological agony of hell is brought about because God allows the soul to realize the sinful tendencies it displayed on earth. There the sinner constantly and unrepentantly chose self in preference to God. Now the nature of things revenges itself upon him. God has, so to speak, ratified the selfish will of the soul in hell. It had constantly sought to make itself the total sum of life; now that wish is fulfilled. The soul is immured within itself without any possibility of normal social contact with others. This of course is a terrible fate, but the horror of this state is slow in dawning upon the soul during this life.

For the modern mind, perhaps, the suffering of the loss of God appears as a fairly logical consequence of mortal sin. If the soul has rejected God until the last moment of its consciousness, it would seem only normal that God should reject the soul, or at least prolong the sinner's attitude in hell. But Sacred Scripture indicates still another suffering, the suffering described as fire or the worm. There is great difficulty here. Whereas the soul's separation from God is seen as the natural consequence of mortal sin, the added torment from fire is seen as unnatural. The difficulty is mitigated if the fire is conceived, not as the instrument of an angry God, but as a natural concomitant of the interior condition which the soul has produced by a perverse will.

By this we do not mean that fire *is* the interior torment which the soul experiences. Nor do we mean that the fire is only metaphorical. Scripture and Tradition make it certain that fire does exist and does eternally torture the unrepentant soul in hell. It is not merely the soul's remorse or its longing desperation. No, it is evident from the way Scripture speaks of fire that it is something real, outside the sufferer, distinct from him. It is a *cause* of suffering and not the suffering itself which is described as fire in the revealed writings. Evidently it is some created being which tortures the soul.

But what precisely is the nature of this fire? We cannot

conceive it as identical with the fire of this earth, for the soul is an immaterial being and very difficult problems would arise were one to conceive of a material fire such as the fire of this earth bringing suffering to an immaterial soul. (This explanation is not entirely impossible, however, because the reactions between the immaterial soul and the material body, as experienced in this life, could suggest to us a pathway towards an explanation.)

St. Thomas suggests that fire acts upon the soul in hell by binding it to one spot and thus limiting its natural liberty of operation and movement as spirit. Thus fire would be chosen as a material element, an element lowest in the scale of being, to humiliate the spiritual soul by holding it immobile. This is a possible explanation. Still, one may ask why it should be fire which binds man. In this life the fire which we experience not only binds man to one spot, it burns him.

St. Bonaventure suggests that the separated soul in hell suffers from an unremitting hallucination of fire. In this theory the fire would not act upon the soul directly, but would produce intense anguish in the soul, which cannot free itself from its obsession. It is tortured by the presence of fire as if fire attacked it directly. Doubtless the fire of hell is only analogous to the fire of this earth; it must be assumed to cause intense pain resembling the pain caused by earthly fire, but unlike earthly fire, it does not consume its object.

Yet after these explanations have been suggested, the modern mind is left with the difficulty of conceiving that a created being is used as a special instrument for the torture of God's enemies.

Another explanation remains at least possible. An emi-

nent theologian has suggested that the central pain of hell
is somewhat like the pain suffered by a split personality
in this life.[1] The soul which was made for God has sought
in this life to love self, and in hell its free will is eternally
fixed in an interior convulsion. As nature and being it still
must seek God with all the energies of its being. But as
a free being it continues to reject God as it did in life. The
simultaneous natural searching for God and the rejection
of God by his free will set up an interior division which
almost tears his personality apart.

We hear in psychology today a great deal about ambi-
valent feelings, a term used to describe the inner conflict
tearing a neurotic person who is pulled in two directions
at the same time, so that he both loves and hates the same
object. This torment of self-contradiction is equivalent to
the rending of a personality on the level of experience.
The soul in hell, feeling this simultaneous natural love and
free hate for God, is rendered absurd to the very last fiber
of its being. It feels its own self-contradictory impulses as
a splitting of its very personality. We know that the split-
personality, the schizophrenic personality, suffers acutely.
The man on one level believes that he is someone else,
yet retains some obscure notion of his actual identity;
there are, as it were, two personalities, two egos. Thus
two superimposed images of himself are at conflict within
his spirit, and riven by this conflict, he suffers as though
devoured by himself.

Is it possible that the soul in hell would feel this inner
division not only with regard to itself but also with regard
to the God for whom it thirsts with all its being? In one
and the same experience, the whole natural urge of its
being surges towards the fountain of goodness, yet at the

same time it is torn away from God by its will, which is
frozen in its rejection of God. Down to the last experience
of man's being, to the very structure of what he is, is
written a longing for God, a longing which causes the
primary suffering of hell, the suffering of the loss of God.
Thus it is an intimation of God's great love for the soul
which the soul experiences in hell, for the fact that it
suffers such agony by its separation from God proves the
greatness of God's love for souls. He had planned the soul
for Himself, to enjoy Himself, the total good.

There are, then, theologians who believe that God has
created no special instrument of torture for the damned
souls in hell. Rather what He has created is this gloriously
beautiful, intricate and fascinating material universe
which He intended to be the home of the soul in the state
of its final resurrection and which would cause the soul
unending joy. But the soul in hell has throughout its life
insisted upon making *itself* the center of the universe. Now
that it is in hell it sees with unmistakable clarity that the
center of the universe is Christ Himself, but still it continues its attempt to superimpose the image of itself as the
very peak of creation. While on earth this man strove
desperately to make everything revolve about himself:
now he is literally taken prisoner by selfishness, and he
desperately attempts to project the image of himself everywhere.

In attempting this projection upon reality, somewhat
as a madman attempts to project the image of himself
as Napoleon, the soul in hell is tortured by the real material universe which conflicts with the soul's false interpretation of it. Wherever the soul looks it beholds the face
of Christ, but now this seeing is a source of torture, since

it is attempting to substitute for Christ the vision of itself as the center of the world and of time and of history. Every particle of being, everything that is, everything that stands in contradiction to nothingness, is somehow a reflection of the eternal Word of God. The soul in hell, in trying to force the image of itself upon all things, undergoes a torture similar to the anguish experienced by a split personality, as we have seen. The unendurable, continual tension that it experiences wherever it comes into contact with being could be described as a suffering akin to the suffering from material fire; a tension which is absolutely unresolvable and which is caused by everything that exists in the material cosmos.

Thus it may be said that in hell the sinner has succeeded; he has achieved what he strove for on this earth. He had labored mightily to be a center totally separated from others, without love, without charity, without sacrifice for others. Now in hell each soul is a mad center unto itself. In hell each soul is in solitude pushed to totality. The soul exists in solitary confinement walled up within itself, entombed alive within itself.

Thus the soul in hell violates and perverts its own nature in much the same fashion as it perverted and violated its own nature in grave sin on earth. Sin is a self-chosen delusion; and sin and its punishment grow upon the same tree, the tree of selfishness. In hell the sinner discovers that his real world battles forever with the unreal world of his imagination until he goes mad on every point of contact with reality, while he still retains sufficient sanity to know that he is mad.

The damned soul is crushed by the nearness of the loving God. Just as the one sun, without alteration to itself, nourishes one plant and burns another, so the same fiery love of God gives joy to the saints in heaven, purifies the souls in purgatory and tortures the souls in hell—with no change in God. In face of God's love, it is evident that the sinner should torture himself to the most intense degree. The pain of fire is thus a complement of the pain of loss and results from the sinner's inner state and the material universe.

Hell is, then, as we have said, far more the work of man than of God. Hell is the work of a man to whom Love Itself, God, has become unbearable. All through Christian art, when the Last Judgment is represented, we see some suggestion of this great truth, for it is the same loving Christ who sends the sinner to hell and the saint to heaven. It is not as though God had suddenly tired of the role of the Redeemer and the Good Shepherd that He took upon Himself in this life. Christ does not play a role. Christ is a redeemer by essence, by His very constitution as God and man. The change is not in God, in whom there is no shadow of alteration. The change is in the hate-filled soul of one who is confronted with infinite love.[2]

We think in our human fashion that God could have arranged things in a more humane way. But as long as God is God, as long as He retains His infinite lovableness and attractiveness, His presence will torture the kind of soul that is in hell. God is not arbitrary, as we are. Rather He is infinitely loving, and if hell is His creation it is a creation which flows from both His justice and His love.

Hell is really contained in the sin itself; hell is the very law of sin carried to its logical conclusion. The very attitude of soul which constitutes a sinner a sinner defines his torture in hell. Hell lets all the negativity of sin itself appear. As sin has been a break with God, with the world, and with others, now, in conflict with itself, the soul in hell realizes to the fullest extent this triple rupture. God has made eternal the choice which the sinner has refused to retract in his life.

Hence the soul in hell cannot look upon its punishment as chosen by a positive, vindictive decree of God; it realizes that the punishment is simply the final disharmony between itself and God and the created universe. Now the sinner is at last aware of the consequences of his chosen rejections of God. On earth the just man says to God, "Thy will be done." The sinner refuses this reverence to God. Now it is God who, with a kind of tragic rightness, says to him, "Thy will be done."

One further question remains: How can men be happy in heaven while they know that others are in hell? How can God Himself be happy in heaven when some of His creatures are in hell? It is not easy to answer this, for it is part of the mystery of hell itself. But it is true to say that the creature in hell has rejected God and the universe by becoming a law unto himself. God in turn must stand in total opposition to the soul who rejects Him. We should not interpret hell as if it were a denial of the opportunity to repent his crime to a sinner who willed to do so. There is no possibility of repentance here. At every moment the sinner maintains that positive attitude of rejection which he struck at the moment of death. He is not sorry for his crime; he is the rebel forever.

It is also true to say that the sinner has lost all solidarity with the world of heaven and of goodness. His hatred cuts him off from the human family whose union consoles us in this life and in heaven.

If we look at hell in this fashion, if we grant the meaning of sin, and the meaning of the torture of hell, we will see that hell is the final and ultimate proof of the greatness of God's love, because the extent of torture in hell reveals the extent of happiness that God had planned for the sinner, who chose to frustrate his own happiness and, so choosing, has been allowed his choice.

# 7

# RESURRECTION

In the Old Testament the notion of a Resurrection is infrequently explored. There are passages, however, that proclaim the omnipotence of God, the Lord of history. Since He is the all-powerful Creator of heaven and earth and of all life upon the earth, surely *sheol* can put up no lasting barrier against Him. It is true that when the earlier biblical books suggest that man may ultimately be released from the power of *sheol* this is really no more than a declaration of faith in that God who will grant long life to man and postpone death-dealing illness. Ancient Israel believed that God would ransom her from the grim bondage of *sheol*, but by this she often understood only that God would grant length of days to the just. Thus she asserted that God would not abandon her in *sheol* but would show her the path of life; but this affirmation was, in effect, a prayer for a long and fruitful temporal career.

Men of today are perhaps surprised to learn that these people, with their high ethical ideals and their noble monotheism, had so little certitude of immortality. This of course can be partially explained by the fact that the idea of community plays, as we have seen, so large a role in Israel's thought. The lack of personal immortality was compensated for by perpetuation through one's descendants. A man could project his future into his children and their children; his name would continue in them and the memory of his fidelity to God would be preserved. When an ancient Israelite considered the history of his nation, his thought turned to its future and he found a vicarious fulfillment in the thought of his people's promised glory. This was the way that God wanted it, and this would suffice for a devout Hebrew. Further, the Jews' inability to conceive of a spirit separate from the body hampered the development of a doctrine such as that of immortality. As we have seen, the concept of a separated soul appears very late in Israelitic thought and probably had Hellenistic origins, whereas the earlier notions of immortality were part of the surrounding Semitic culture.

It is, then, in the prophetic books that the theme of the resurrection is first clearly heard, and it is not easy to separate the affirmations of the Prophets from the hyperbolic and metaphorical language in which they are so brilliantly clothed. The difficulty is compounded, too, because the Prophets often unite conceptions which properly refer to the restoration of Israel with those which refer in some way to the resurrection of the individual. The vision of Ezechiel, in which he speaks of God re-animating the corpses of his people and clothing the dry bones with living flesh, seems entirely directed to the future kingdom of Israel and not to any literal resurrection of the dead as individuals. Isaias also speaks of a moment in the future when the sovereign power of Yahweh will be attested by His power over death. Death will be annihilated by His all-powerful hand, but this expression seems rather an emphatic way of declaring that when Israel submits to the saving will of the Lord golden peace and prosperity will shower upon her from His hand.

The book of Daniel, however, makes quite clear that those who suffer martyrdom for persecution and are deprived of glory on earth will awaken in an everlasting dawn where the aureole of their courage will cause them to shine like stars forever. The inhabitants of *sheol* will return to life, some indeed to their ignominy, but others to be exalted because of the witness they have borne to their faith in the immortal God. God will eventually overthrow the gray realm of death and re-establish a kingdom of the living, of those risen from the dead. Through all her history Israel had accounted as supremely important the acceptance of Yahweh's sovereign will. Now, in her later epoch, she perceives that even the conquest of death is possible to God and will take place for those who have submitted to His will in faith.

We find this sort of confidence echoed by the seven stalwart brothers of the second book of Machabees. Their spirits are stiffened throughout their sufferings by the constant belief in a Messianic era when the Lord will raise them in triumph. As the reward of obedience the King of the universe will grant them in that day a risen life far richer than the present one. The tortured limbs will be restored and the valiant mother will recover her sons, her triumphant faith fulfilled. The sacrifice of Judas in the second book of Machabees indicates the same belief in an eventual resurrection of the body, though in this conviction there is still a blending of collective and individual perspectives.

## THE TEACHING OF THE NEW TESTAMENT

In the New Testament, of course, all obscurity is dissolved. Jesus decisively informs the Sadducees that the power of God will effect the Resurrection and reminds them that had they known the Scriptures they would have found indications of this fact. The Living God will restore those who have lived by His life while on earth. Martha, for instance, is a herald of the Christian faith in Jesus as the Resurrection and the Life for those who have committed themselves to Him in faith. The great proof, however, is the resurrection of Christ Himself, the Head of the human race, and therefore subsequent Christian preaching rarely separates the two themes of Christ's resurrection and our own.

The fact that Jesus always linked the prediction of His death with that of His resurrection is obvious from the testimony of His enemies. They reminded Pilate that Jesus had said: "After three days I will arise." Our Lord Himself on the road to Emmaus insisted upon the necessity of His death and resurrection as He expounded for the disciples the biblical tradition on these matters. Moreover, it is Jesus Himself who constantly relates His death and resurrection to ours. This is done, for instance, at the institution of the Holy Eucharist, which the disciples are to celebrate until His return. The mysteries of the Lord of Salvation are also the mysteries of His Mystical Body.

The fact of the Resurrection is, then, the foundation stone of Christianity, even as it gave ultimate meaning to Our Lord's whole life. If Christ is not risen, then we shall not rise and our faith is vain. But if Christ is risen, then our hope is founded in believing that He is the firstborn from among the dead and that we too shall rise in glory with Him. St. Paul insists upon this at Athens. There he unites our resurrection to the resurrection of Christ, and later in Jerusalem, in his discourse before the Sanhedrin, he will again insist on the two themes. When he speaks before the governor, Felix, or King Agrippa he once more renders testimony both to the resurrection of Christ and to ours, for the former is a pledge of the latter.

The resurrection in which Christians believe is dramatically foreshadowed immediately after Our Lord's death: "And behold the veil of the temple was rent in two from the top even to the bottom: and the earth quaked and the rocks were rent. And the graves were opened: and many bodies of the saints that had slept arose, and coming out of the tombs after his resurrection, came into the holy city and appeared to many" (Matt. xxvii, 51-3). The resurrection of Christ, as this episode proves, is already active in His Mystical Body, although its total significance will not appear until the last day when the grave gives up all its dead. In the Synoptics this episode of the resurrection of the bodies of the just is used along with the resurrection of Lazarus to exemplify Jesus' power of resurrection and to teach us that it will be prolonged and developed in humanity as part of His victory over death.

The moving speech of Peter on Pentecost again bears witness to the resurrection of Jesus. Immediately after speaking on this great theme Peter cures the paralytic, thereby linking resurrection in Christ's Mystical Body to the resurrection of Jesus Himself. As the paralytic leaps up to new life, so will all the faithful members of Christ rise on the last day to confront triumphantly the face of their victorious Leader who has preceded them in the conquest of death.

It is by this sort of light that we must understand the Christian's death. All the lines of theology concerning death converge in the Paschal mystery of Jesus' cross and resurrection, His passage to the Father. Since Baptism is our entrance into the death and resurrection of Jesus, it holds a uniquely important place in the life of the early Christian community. St. Paul in fact tells us that at Corinth the practice had been introduced of baptizing the dead by proxy in order to assure for them the benefits of the resurrection of Jesus. The Eucharist is likewise closely connected with the resurrection because it brings us into communion with the risen Lord and sows in us the beginning of eternal life. In fact the entire sacramental system bears very intimately upon the death and resurrection of Jesus and the death to sin and the resurrection to life that Jesus' members must share. Through these sacraments, indeed, the victory of Jesus works itself out in time to the ultimate hour of total fulfillment.

## THE RESURRECTION IN CHRISTIAN THOUGHT

When we turn from these biblical perspectives to our own day we find that many of our contemporaries approach the thought of a resurrection of the body with a certain uneasiness. The philosophic temper of the twentieth century does not easily accommodate the idea that the creative power of God will summon back to existence the composite man, body and soul. And of course this doctrine must do violence to any purely speculative framework, since our belief in the resurrection is neither derived from nor supported by philosophy. The resurrection will come about, not through any power of development inherent in man's nature, but by the powerful will of the most high God, who herewith fulfills those native aspirations of man for which there is no natural explanation.

The Christian Church manifestly defends here a humanism far more extensive in its importance and depth than any natural humanism could pretend to be. Throughout its history the Church has been an eloquent pleader for man, man as he is constituted by God, body and soul, and his rights, privileges and dignities have been consistently stressed. Other groups have felt that they were guarding human liberties when they overemphasized one or other aspect of man's nature, but man as a unit is defended validly only when all his interests are defended in the just measure that is due to each of them.

History has known some calling themselves Christians who were concerned exclusively with defending man as a spirit. God in His creative wisdom, however, made man a composite, enfleshed spirit; an incarnate spirit; a spirit capable of expressing itself only in and through that matter which it dominates, forms and shapes and which becomes for it an instrument capable of spiritual expression. In the Christian framework man's destiny is human, the destiny not of a spirit but of a man composed of both body and spirit.

For this reason the Christian Church says little about the activity of the separated soul. At least, one could say, the ancient Christian tradition rarely speaks of the separated soul. Its activities after death remain mysterious, and the Church has not elaborated any formal dogma in this regard. She has said very clearly that the soul which has fulfilled the total will of the Lord goes at once to heaven and the beatific vision. But she has not told us how the soul functions without its natural companion, the body. The interest of the Christian Church is rather always with the total man.

At the solemn ending of the Apostle's Creed we are astonished to find a resounding reference to mortal man: "I believe in the resurrection of the body." At the close of all those majestic phrases which were hammered out through centuries of theological controversies we find a precise declaration about man as man, body and soul— indeed the emphasis seems to be upon the body. The intellectual toil of early Councils was devoted to formulating the dogmas of the oneness of God, the Trinity, the mystery of Creation and the immeasurable depths of the mystery of the Incarnation. And suddenly, from these dizzying heights the Creed descends to this unexpected,

almost anti-climactic statement: "I believe in the resurrection of the body." Man with all his miseries and all his
imperfections, his sins, his omissions, his tragic-comic history suddenly looms up at the close of this profession of
faith.

It is anti-climactic, however, only for one who does not
understand the utter centrality of the Paschal mystery: the
passage of Christ to His Father by death and resurrection
is at the heart of every Christian mystery. This is the focus
from which life flows and unity emerges for every dogma
of the Christian faith. It has been stated repeatedly that
the Paschal mystery of Christ is inseparable from the
death and resurrection of His Church. The triumph of
Christ will not be complete until His entire Church has
risen and His glory is seen in all of His members. Throughout history God, the Eternal Father, has prepared the birth
of this new humanity, this Mystical Body of the Lord.
Throughout His redemptive life Christ Himself labored
to this end, and the redemption of this new body was
virtually accomplished when He rose from the dead. For
at that moment the sacrifice of Our Lord was declared
accepted by the Father and a new existence began upon
this earth, the existence of Christ prolonged in space and
time.

Yet there are many Christians who have never quite
grasped the meaning of the Incarnation upon which their
faith is founded. They think of the Incarnation in terms
of a necessary condition for a juridical redemption. But
the Church teaches much more than this. At the moment
of the Incarnation our redemption was begun and sem-
inally accomplished. When Christ joined Himself to hu-

manity He began at once the great healing process of redemption. He poured Himself, as it were, into the wounds of broken humanity.

By His divinizing contact this Man, who was in a certain sense Universal Man, re-created existent humanity, and there is today in heaven a human material body which is adorable. There is a body, a truly human body like my own, which is the object of the adoration one offers to God alone. This is the body of the Word. Does this not stir me to a fresh appreciation of the value of matter? That cult which is reserved exclusively to the Lord of the universe is now given to one of our race, of our own human family. Once we have grasped this fact the entire conception of the material world and of the significance of the body radically shifts. The depths here are vast, and many who have bent over them have felt their heads swim. One must recall the axiom of the Fathers: "Remaining what He was He assumed what He was not." The immaterial and eternally perfect God who had dwelt for all eternity in inaccessible light assumed into personal union with Himself a material body and a human soul. This is a truth that one must try to penetrate in order to understand the destiny that Christianity opens up for the body.

Some of the early Christians protested against this truth. It so far surpassed the demands and the possibilities which their philosophies opened to them that they could not believe that the body of Christ actually came from this earth, that its origin was ultimately from Adam. They protested that it was a heavenly body, and that it had passed through the body of the Virgin Mary merely as through a mode of entry into this world.

But the entire Christian Church rose in unison at that time and thundered "No" to this aberration. The Church rang with the indignant protestation that Mary was in very truth the Mother of God, that she had prepared the material of Christ's body from her own. It is well that the Church showed this concern, for at that moment our whole future as men was at stake. Other early Christians who could not grasp the divinization and the redemption of matter claimed that God would contaminate Himself by assuming it into a personal union. They concluded that Christ had assumed only the appearance of a material body, something which would be useful to Him in dealing with men, but which would not in any sense render Him human. But the Church declared that Christ's body was truly material, not just apparently so. Moreover, it was dust of this earth, derived from the family of Adam; consequently there was established a blood kinship between God and Man. Were this not true, our future as men would be illusory, for any immortality of the soul would simply mean that the human person as such disappears. A human person is a combination of body and soul. Christ redeemed only what He assumed, and if He did not assume a body, then our body is doomed to everlasting corruption and death, to return to the elements from which it was made.

It is, then, sometimes necessary to remind Christians that theirs is not a faith in the immortality of the soul. The doctrine of the immortality of the soul has, to be sure, an ancient lineage. A long tradition in Grecian thought culminating in Plato argues this theme, and there are metaphysical and philosophical reasonings designed to prove that the soul is by its nature immortal. As a spiritual being, incapable of corruption from within or from without, it is susceptible of annihilation at the hands of God, but it is not susceptible to natural death. Any able philosopher can demonstrate that without appeal to Christianity. It has ever been Christianity's concern not primarily to prove the immortality of the soul but to confront man with her own vision: the resurrection of total man, body and soul, redeemed in Christ. What God has revealed is not the everlasting life of the soul but of man himself.

How surprising it is, therefore, to find among Christians a tendency to ignore the importance of the risen body. This of course is a wholly inadequate view of Christian revelation. To insist upon the immortality of the soul at the expense of Christian revelation concerning the body is to rob human history of its depth. Any happiness which excludes the body, any happiness planned for man in a bodiless existence, is in some sense defective, since it is not fully human. We know that the soul which has pleased God utterly enjoys the beatific vision, which is the essential happiness of heaven. But expectation remains, for the soul still awaits the resurrection of its body. Only then will the man be completely himself in the unity of the entire Christian community, where all are fully themselves in their resurrected bodies.

No one hesitates to say that the soul is more important than the body, but the body too has its value. That is why in this life we chastise it and train it to be a faithful companion and docile instrument. In the light of Christian wisdom anyone who believed that he was becoming more holy by despising the body would be in grave error. Twenty centuries of theology bear witness to the fact that as soon as a Christian sect teaches contempt of the body, its next step in practice is into unbounded license. And this license is completely logical, for if the body is contemptible, it may be allowed to do what it will. Then are refounded the Corinth and the Rome which St. Paul described.

"It is not the body that counts but the soul," certain Christians have said. But Christ did not die to redeem a soul; he died to redeem men, and men are not constituted by soul alone.

We wonder what this resurrected body will be like. Certainly it will be much more fully one's own than that possessed on earth. The soul, liberated by grace, will dominate this body more completely, and the body will lend itself willingly to such domination. As a result it will be more personalized, more individualized, more expressive of him who possesses it than was the earthly body.

It will be spiritual, pneumatic, but this is not to imply that it will fail to possess that solidity, that substantiality, that denseness of reality which we associate with matter. On the contrary, this body will have acquired a new facility for expressing the soul. Whereas in the past, matter resisted the self-expression of the spirit, now it will yield itself up to the desires of the soul and the wishes, the thoughts, the decisions of the self will be mirrored in the body with an ease and a transparency that would astonish us now.

Although Christian thought finds it hard to describe this new habitation, revelation makes it clear that this will be the same body we owned on earth. That appears to us quite natural, since our body is an inalienable part of our identity. It is also clear that this will be a body perfected by the power of God, who created it originally and who now re-creates it to respond to the needs of the purified soul in heaven.

We can say of this body that it will be the ultimate in corporeal perfection. It will be matter come to its triumph, matter come to its term. Its supreme model will be those two bodies at this moment reigning gloriously in heaven: the resurrected body of Christ Himself, the first man in the new line of manhood which began at Calvary, and the body of Mary, assumed in triumph to share the triumph of her Son.

In this new state the body will realize all the corporal potentialities that are now scarcely suspected. For instance, it is the very perfection of matter to be submissive to the spirit, as St. Thomas teaches us. The matter of this body will therefore express the spirit, will yield to the spirit with ease and with joy. It will not be the crass, burdensome, dull, impenetrable, expressionless matter that we find, for instance, in rocks. It will not possess the drag of matter, the inertia that so often affects us now and acts as a weight or downward pull upon our soul. We know from experience in this life how weary our body can be and how a weary body affects the spirit, dulls the sharp edge of intelligence, blunts the edge of desire in the will, puts up a smoke screen before the imagination and slows down the whole spiritual mechanism of man. We know that a fatigued body can cause the spirit to live in a sort of fog-bound atmosphere in which right and wrong are no longer clearly distinguished, truth and falsehood seem to lose their sharp borders.

There are even times in this life when the body seems to celebrate a triumph over the spirit in that it refuses to be made subject to the spirit and executes its will independently of it. Such stubborn resistance will not be possible with the resurrected body.

This new, risen body will be like an instrument in the hands of a master. The risen body will be the soul's most docile instrument, and it will reveal all the hidden harmonics of expression of the soul, yielding itself to the soul's slightest wish, so that at long last the perfect image of the soul's life will have been evolved.

It is clear that such a mystery could not result from any interior gift of the body itself nor from any interior gift of the risen immortal soul. It is as a direct reply to the creative God, the source of all being, that the new body will take its shape, its color, its characteristics. It is difficult for us to derive, from our partial grasp of human experience, analogies to convey the nature of spiritualized, personalized matter. And yet there are such analogies even in this life. It is possible for us to distinguish within matter, even as we see it on this earth, various forms and degrees of submissiveness to spirit.

When we pass, for example, from the animal world to the human we see at once that matter has taken a giant step towards spiritualization. A newborn child may be very much like a small animal in many ways, yet it is also marvelously different. Matter submits here to a higher principle, and becomes personalized. As time passes any mother will notice the gradual extension of the personal principle as the body yields itself up to be dominated by and to express spirit.

And within the human realm itself matter is susceptible of many gradations in spirituality. Think of the face of a noble character, who lives in the world of values and in communion with things which have an importance in themselves. The countenance and the very bodily movements of such a man reflect his spiritual environment in an entirely new way. The photographer who looks for interesting faces does not always seek them among the young or even among the beautiful. Instead he searches for a transparent face in which matter has gained an extraordinary freedom to express the spirit. This is one of the gifts of a great actor or great actress, this mobility of the body's response to the nobility of spirit. The face in a generally intellectual and spiritual person can be more beautiful at ninety than it was at nineteen, for there is a power of evocation in a face dominated finally by an intellectual spirit that is not found in the most perfect formal beauty of youth. The fact is that matter in the human person is far more humanized, more personalized, more subtle, mobile, free, than matter encountered in the non-human world. It has become genuinely an instrument for the spirit.

Thus it is not entirely unintelligible, even to unaided human reason, that matter in the resurrected body should be what theologians call pneumatic, spiritual. The body which was sown as a heavy material body, earthy, crass, will rise as an expression of the spirit. Theologians also point out, following Sacred Scripture, that the new bodies of the risen Christians will be immortal. They will no longer be susceptible to death nor to the preparations for death which we know as suffering and sickness. This corruption will have put on incorruption and this mortality will have put on immortality. In this body there will be no defect. All will be perfect beauty, and the very perfection of beauty includes an immense variety.

The new body of the risen man will also shine with that clarity and glory which is proper to heaven. The soul will irradiate through the body as light irradiates through a crystal. The body in heaven will also be what theologians call subtle—it will be utterly docile to the soul. It will obey the will with the speed of light, for bodies sown in weakness will rise in power.

One wonders also whether in some fashion the history of all the temporal experiences of this person will not be recorded in the risen body. For to the Christian who cherishes deeply the events and happenings of human life it cannot but seem likely that these should be reflected in some fashion in the risen man, and that the pneumatic body will have the power to express the total man with all of the decisive options of his past, all of his triumphs, sufferings, liberations, all the effects of grace as it was radicated in the human person who he is. Impregnated with history, the body holds in unity the endless experiences of man's temporal journey.

And what will be the limits of the body? Once it functioned in terms of other things—hands made use of tools. Through our bodies we were related to other things in this life, for they plunged us into the world of matter, change and history. We were incarnated in a particular time and a particular culture; everything that has touched and formed the destiny of man in time will somehow be assumed in a fresher, newer form in eternity.

Doubtless we can say that in some transcendent fashion these material and spiritual entities will be registered in the Kingdom of Heaven in relationship to the resurrected body. We must not limit the power of the Lord. We must not ignore the meaning of time and of human history and of all that goes into the making of the story of a soul. But we must also beware of projecting our imaginations beyond the limits that revelation has indicated to us.

# 8

# HEAVEN

Heaven is our fatherland, and there is our true home. Its essential splendor is that eternal vision of God, face-to-face, which is itself the beatifying source of our endless happiness. All this, of course, is a mystery which the eye of man cannot penetrate, the depths of which his ear cannot sound nor his mind surmise. However, our human reason aided by the light of revelation can form some fragmentary idea of what heaven is like. Sacred Scripture, for instance, often indicates that eternal life is a recompense towards which the soul must tend. It suggests, besides, that the glory which will render us everlastingly happy in heaven is the same glory which—and here we must fall back on human terms—has rendered God infinitely happy with no shadow of boredom or ennui throughout eternity.

## KNOWLEDGE AND LOVE

In this world the Christian life is still imperfect but destined to develop to perfect fullness. This present state of infancy strains towards maturity. Our knowledge of God in this life is confused and partial. Because it is drawn from creatures it is obscure and indirect, quite unlike that other awareness which St. Paul calls, in Hebrew fashion, "face-to-face" knowledge because it involves an immediate intuition of the adorable Trinity. In his Second Epistle to the Corinthians, chapter v, verses 6 to 8, St. Paul bids us take courage: while we are in this material body we are far from the Lord; we walk in faith and not by vision; but one day we will dwell close to the Lord. We cannot now see the glories of Christ, for this is a privilege reserved for the elect, but the time will come when every faithful Christian will be gladdened by this intuitive vision of Christ and of God.

St. John proclaims the same truth in his First Epistle, chapter iii, verses 1 and 2. The beloved apostle recalls first of all the great love with which the Father has graced us, so that we can be called and truly be the children of God. Our divine sonship is a participation in the unique natural sonship of Jesus. Because it is such a participation, it gives a right to the heritage of the Father, and St. John tells us what this implies: "Beloved," he says, "we are sons of God even now, and what we shall be hereafter, has not been made known to us as yet. But we know that when he comes we shall be like him; we shall see him, then, as he is."

The Church in turn repeats this consoling doctrine. In the constitution *Benedictus Deus,* for instance, Benedict XII infallibly sums up the scriptural and traditional teachings concerning the happiness of the elect. "They will see the divine essence with an intuitive and face-to-face vision, without the intermediary of any creature, but immediately, thanks to the divine essence which manifests itself to them clearly and openly."

Naturally the human soul is incapable of any such face-to-face vision of God by its own forces. But God can elevate it by the infusion of a gift which we call the light of glory. This so expands the intelligence that the soul can directly gaze upon the uncreated beauty of the Godhead and in that intuitive vision be most intimately united to God.

Indeed, the interior activity of God Himself consists precisely in self-knowledge and self-love, and when the human soul knows and loves God in the intuitive vision it shares this divine interior life. God is endlessly and infinitely happy in knowing and loving Himself because knowledge and love are in Him the plenitude of being. In similar fashion, the happiness of the blessed soul is scarcely imaginable. To behold God as He is in Himself is to grasp God in Himself; to possess the full idea of God is to possess God Himself. There is between the soul in heaven and the Godhead a very close union, somewhat like that which exists between an idea and the mind which conceives it.

The first object of the intuitive vision is thus God Himself, and the happiness of heaven consists above all in this vision. The greater the knowledge which the soul has of God, the greater will be its love and the greater will be its glory. In looking upon the divine essence face-to-face the soul will know all the divine attributes and the three divine Persons who are identified with this Divine Essence. It will not, therefore, contemplate God in a series of fragmentary acts but will behold the whole of the Godhead in all its essential perfections and in its adorable Trinity. Nevertheless, God will remain incomprehensible; not in the sense that there is something in Him which will not be seen but in the sense that He will not be seen as perfectly as He sees Himself.

Moreover, the Blessed in heaven will also have a certain knowledge of creatures, in God. In the Divine Essence, in which God Himself knows all things, will be unveiled for them certain truths touching creation. For God, who is the universal and transcendent cause, contains within Himself a representation of all those things which are distinct from Himself. In heaven we will contemplate in the Divine Essence whatever can interest or legitimately concern us. The mirror of the Divine Essence will be opened for the Blessed.

The mysteries of the faith which we have believed upon this earth will now be clearly manifested. We shall understand all that concerns the Church as a supernatural society; the efficacy of the Sacraments; the real presence of Jesus in the Eucharist; and the admirable fashion in which Providence has conducted us to our eternal destiny. Because the elect have once lived in this created world they will know its marvels in heaven insofar as these will be interesting to them or useful to increase their love and gratitude. How extensive will that knowledge be? It is hard to tell, but St. Thomas says that it will wholly fulfill the soul's natural desires. Because the Just in heaven know the things that interest them upon earth St. Thomas assures us that the saints have an immediate intuition of our prayers.

The depth of our knowledge and love in heaven and the degree of our glory will correspond to the intensity of charity which animated us while still on earth. The soul will also quite naturally retain the ideas which it elaborated painfully and carefully here below. Moreover, the blessed souls retain the memory of the events of their human life, of the persons who were their companions on the journey towards the homeland, and of their own affections and struggles.

Of course, those souls who arrive in heaven with a certain natural immaturity—for example, children who have never reached the age of reason or adults who have not developed their intelligence—will receive at that moment from God a certain correction, in the natural order, of this deficiency. In heaven there will be no conflict in our human will, there will be no possibility of sadness. Even before the Resurrection, the soul will not experience any suffering at the lack of union with its body. Having everything that it can desire in the total good of the Godhead, the soul will be satisfied, although it does not yet possess its glory in all the completeness which God intends.

Nothing can trouble the peaceful intimacy of God and the soul, neither the regret for those who are still absent from the company of the Just nor compassion for those who have for eternity rendered themselves unworthy of the Divine Presence. Moreover, the elect will derive great joy from the presence of those who are with them in heaven, for they will have direct communication with other members of the heavenly court.

We cannot suppose that they will communicate with one another only through the Divine Essence. Rather we must expect that they will exercise their proper faculties, and love and know one another in heaven through these faculties. Charity will have reached in them the supreme degree of the perfection of which they are capable, and they will love one another with the most ardent and tender love, a love which will be constantly nourished by the perfect knowledge which they possess of the natural and supernatural perfections of each other.[1]

The joys that are proper to the resurrected body are mysterious ones. We know that the glory of the soul will react upon the body. We can here note simply that the reunion of soul and body will [reconstitute the organic faculties of the body.) Doubtless in these sensible bodily faculties there will be a new element of joy for the soul. Our eyes and our ears, we can easily understand, will be gladdened by the sights which meet them in heaven and the sounds which accompany that life. As regards the less spiritual senses of smell, touch, and taste, it is not so easy for us to understand in what fashion they add to the accidental glory of the soul in heaven, but that they do we do not doubt.

## THE LIFE OF GLORY

The Divine Life which God planted in our souls at our entrance into the Church through Baptism now develops and shows its full profundity and mysterious power. For glory is really a prolongation of grace, as grace is the seed of glory. The term which occurs so often in Scripture indicates this, for Scripture calls heaven "eternal life."

This phrase intimates that the life led there flows into our souls as the consequence of the eternal life already implanted at Baptism and nourished by the sacraments. The life of the human spirit here on earth is always subject to the flight of time. It cannot develop all its powers by a single act but must creep along by a continual succession of distinct, repeated acts. But the life of the spirit living in God is somewhat like the Divine Life, for it is truly eternal. The soul now knows and loves God, in and through Himself, and in doing so it embraces God in a single act of knowledge and love which endures for eternity.

The joy of the saints, therefore, is complete because they have reached the fulfillment of their nature, the ultimate expansion of their possibilities for life. The purpose of our existence is everlasting joy, and all our human effort in this world is aimed at obtaining that joy. Heaven will be a harmonious fulfillment of that quest, but for this fulfillment the Creator must raise the potential of man above its natural level to the point where it can share in the joy of God Himself. It is of this complete development that the Lord speaks when He says to His disciples, "I have said these things that my joy may be in you and that your joy may be perfect." God supplies what man lacks. God fulfills and completes what man has begun on earth.

One often wonders if there will be progress and an evolution of happiness in heaven. There will not be progress, because heaven is the infinite attainment of all our hopes, even the hope of progress itself. The essential glory

of heaven will be realized in this perfect beatific fulfillment of the man himself in the supernatural union with
God. The intelligence perceives God and the heart is
thrilled with love. While on earth we are in exile because
we are destined for a fullness of life which cannot maintain
itself upon this earth. We already bear within ourselves
the grace of that glory, but we have not here a lasting city.
In the end we are destined for a glory which is commen-
surate with no creature because it is proper to God Himself.

The totality of life which God will give to us in heaven
surpasses all the dimensions of this world. The contempla-
tion of the unveiled majesty of God is a flowering of a
completely new dimension of life, and if it is a new dimension of life it will also be a new dimension of love. The
final meaning of our lives is always found in life itself.
*"Vita mutatur non tollitur,"* life is changed, it is not taken
away. With Christ the last word is *life*.

Heaven will be the ultimate and consummate perfection
of our poor, torn being which here on earth suffered so
many divisions, even to the division within the soul itself.
In heaven the soul will enjoy total and untroubled, active
peace. There will be no grief or wailing, for God Himself
will wipe away all tears. It is not easy for us to describe
this life, but we know it is not static, for life is defined
as a capacity for action. We know that it is the fulfillment
of all our tendencies, the completion of ourselves, the
plenitude of joy. In heaven God Himself will exert His
inexhaustible energy to raise the soul of the elect to this
capacity for joy. He will labor and take thought to gladden
the human heart.

This is no bodiless and dim existence like the *sheol* of

the Jews. This is no impersonal survival, for the human person will never have been so completely himself. It will be the uninterrupted gazing upon the infinite beauty that is God. St. John Chrysostom said of hell that "ten thousand times ten thousand hells of popular imagination could not equal the grief that the loss of this vision would cause for one moment." We will be taken up as citizens of the new Jerusalem, and upon us will be written His name and the name of the city of God.

We will love and we will be loved; the word will take on all the depth of meaning which we did not find in it in this life. Everything that is lovable and beautiful in human life and in human love will be present here in its concentrated essence. More intense, more complete a fulfillment of man cannot be conceived, for there is no limit to the power of God to love, and there is no limit to His power to deliver Himself to us except the limits we have imposed by our own unwillingness to live as He has planned.

It is obviously impossible for us to explain the mystery of this beatifying vision of God. It is impossible because of the infinity of God Himself, which exceeds the finite by the innermost nature of its being and does not belong to any category at all. God is unique and incomparable. He stands by Himself alone, the totally Other.

No creature therefore can by its natural powers see God as He is. We are like God only as the reflection is like the reality. We image His infinite beauty in distant and shadowy fashion, and only His creative power can bridge the distance between us. Infinite though God is, He could not create a being for whom this beatific vision would be natural. Nor is there any magic in death which would change the nature of our deepest intellect and remove its natural incapacity for that divine reward which comes as pure gift. The beatific vision, indeed, will be the sight of God without any sense-image or any thought-image intervening. God Himself, in a mysterious fashion, will play the role which in our natural process of understanding is played by an idea. He will render Himself immediately intelligible to our minds by uniting Himself to those minds. He will from within the mind itself be known and grasped. When this takes place the heart of man's being will thrill in unison with the divine life and man will come to an awakened consciousness. The soul's knowledge, restricted in this life by the conditions of the body, will develop and be set free to a new mode of knowledge, the knowledge of glory.

One has but to think of the highest moral beauty he has experienced upon this earth, the most dearly beloved person whom he knows, and then to realize that moral beauty raised to the infinite is what he will contemplate in heaven. And the love that exists between the elect in heaven and their God is a mutual love. Heaven is not a passive state, nor is God merely an object which is contemplated. He is personal to the depths of His innermost being, and He returns eternally the soul's gaze of love.

The transports of this spiritual love will be of an intensity that it is impossible for the soul in its present condition to imagine. The more perfect the love, the more total the surrender of the lover to the beloved, and the love of God for the Christian soul is most perfect. We realize, then, that He must deliver himself over to the elect in heaven with an intensity and an intimacy which is inconceivable to us in this life. This love of God, this reciprocal love between God and man, will constitute the total satisfaction of all human desire.

## CHRIST AND CREATION

Before His ascension into heaven Christ spoke the following words: "Behold, I am with you all days, even to the consummation of the world." And He has kept His promise. When He ascended into heaven Our Lord did not withdraw Himself from our human history but continued to act within it, giving it dynamism towards its term. He remained engaged in the battle of humanity and of the universe. His solidarity with man was not broken by His ascension, for he remained within humanity as a pledge of its final victory. The redemptive activity of Christ occupies the whole of human history from the first moments after Adam's fall until the salvation of the last of the elect. It is a divine labor which will be continued until the end of time.

This action of God, in Christ, upon humanity entered into its last phase with the Incarnation and the redemptive sacrifice of the Cross. The entire being of Jesus is redemptive; He is constituted Savior by His very nature as God-man. At the moment that He became man the whole of human history was re-oriented towards the salvation of humanity, and the sacrifice of the Cross is the decisive moment in this history.

It is the action of Christ inscribing itself in history through the activity of individuals which we usually consider when we think of the redemptive activity of Christ. The individual is buried and risen with Christ and participates thus in the continued mystery of the Redemption. But the whole of humanity is on the march toward the actualization by the whole body of Christ of this salvific death and resurrection first enacted upon Calvary. It is for this purpose that the Risen Christ remains present to humanity, engaged in the human drama, the agent of the victory of His Mystical Body. He is not an accidental factor in human history; rather He is the turning point and the spring of human history.

History prepared for His coming, and the meaning of history before His advent derives entirely from Him. By the mystery of His Incarnation He plunged himself irrevocably into the world of time and matter. By doing so He has become the center upon which turns the whole meaning of the cosmos.

It is a temptation to us to minimize the reality of the Incarnation and the consequences which flow from the fact that Christ is united with our race and with our earth. History works itself out upon this center which is Christ, and it is He who gives meaning to all the forms of culture and civilization, all the riches and discoveries of science throughout time and space. His salvific action is deployed in all these earthly realities.

Now the earth which humanity inhabits is one of the prime realities for humanity, and it too has its part in the Redemption. This entire world in which we live is destined to be transformed so that it will be a fitting home for risen humanity.[2]

This world which fell in Adam will rise in Christ. As St. Ambrose says, "The earth too arose in Christ, the heavens too arose in Him." This material universe has been redeemed along with material humanity. As St. Cyril of Jerusalem says, "These skies will pass, but only that lovelier skies appear." And St. Basil comments, "Every earthly creature will be changed along with us." And St. Jerome, commenting on St. Peter, said that St. Peter does not say that we shall see a *different* world in eternity and *different* skies, but "we shall see the same world made glorious."

The Fathers of the Church remind us incessantly that Christ has saved only that which He assumed. But if we are to have an understanding of the dimensions of Our Lord's salvific work, we must extend it beyond the horizon of His individual life into secular and human history. By the fact of His Incarnation Christ became incarnate in a particular culture with a particular accent, language and human way of thinking. These accidental circumstances of time, of place, of culture, of civilization have to be taken into account in any study of the Incarnation. But at the same time we must realize that Christ's purpose is to be incarnated in every century, in every culture, in every civilization. It is the present task of the Christian to incarnate the Lord in the twentieth century, so that His influence extends over the entire field of human activity, discovery, value. This should bring home to the Christian the fact that he is living in a living universe. This does not mean that the material universe about us is gifted with the principle of life and vitality in itself. But what it does imply is that human life, with its intellectual and spiritual character, is profoundly linked with this earthly cosmos of which it is a part and from which it draws its nourishment.

Human life controls much of the universe about it, but it is also sustained by that universe. It emerges from the material world to approach a spiritual climate. But before emerging, human life roots itself in the only cosmos which it knows, the present material cosmos.

Into this universe Christ came as a man among men with a fully human nature, an individual human nature, taken from mankind. His life in this universe was brief, and if one judges it by external success, ineffective, for after some three years of public life He disappeared from the public eye. Because His death, like any death, meant the removal of a sensible presence, there can be a temptation to consider Christ simply a figure of the past.

The Christian, however, must resist this temptation. Christ is not in human history like a seed sown long ago and only destined to fructify little by little after its death. Rather He is insistently present to every moment of time. When we speak of Christ as dead and risen, we do not mean that He has continued to survive as a separated soul escaped from the jaws of death. We mean that He is risen *in His bodily condition* as man, body and soul, although the body is now spiritualized. Our understanding of what it means to have a body should show us that Christ will never lose the bonds which tie Him to our world. What we celebrate on Easter Day is not the fact that the soul of Christ escaped from His body, as it were, to manifest the victory of the spirit over the flesh. Nor do we celebrate the fact that Christ, having met a cruel reception in this world, has departed from it body and soul, content to return to the glory which He had before the Incarnation and to leave this universe to its own devices. Christ does not take up again in heaven the life which He had *before the Incarnation.* He cannot take up that identical life because the Christ who returns to the glory which He possessed from all eternity in the bosom of His Father returns constituted *man, body* and *soul.* The Incarnation of Christ is perpetual, it will not cease for all eternity.

The continual possession of a body by Christ implies much more than this; it suggests that the bonds which unite Him to this world will never be severed because of that body. To the glory of eternity there is now associated a body drawn from this world to which Christ, the *Verbum,* is indissolubly united. This is a necessary consequence of Christ's choice of becoming man and uniting personally the Word of God with a humanity drawn from this material universe.

To conceive of the body of Christ as a mere appearance necessary for His apostolic ministry is an error long since rejected by Christianity. It is equally erroneous to conceive of Christ's body as an instrument necessary for Him during His few active years on earth and dispensed with after death. His body in heaven is glorified and transfigured but it remains genuine, as will our own resurrected body; it is the same body which He possessed upon earth, and because it continues to be an Adamic body, Christ continues to act within humanity and within this world to transform both. Both must be assimilated to Christ, the Head of the new humanity which itself is rooted in this material universe. The Head of the Mystical Body has entered victoriously into heaven and draws after Him progressively all His members, until that day when "we shall reach perfect manhood, that maturity which is proportioned to the completed growth of Christ" (Eph. iv, 13).

The entire universe thus depends and receives its orientation from Christ, who draws it towards that definitive state into which He has already entered. It was never the intention of Christ to proclaim an economy which does no more than reveal the vanity of this earthly existence and our need to detach ourselves from the world. Cer-

tainly He assured us repeatedly of the necessity of detach-
ing ourselves from the "world" in the Johannine sense,
the sinful world which attracts us to evil. But while Christian doctrine exposes the illusion of this false love of the
world it teaches us that we are attached to this world by
bonds which will never be severed. It is precisely that
bondage which gives us a responsibility towards history,
culture, civilization and the material cosmos itself. We
must labor with Christ for His Incarnation in the present.

Christianity, of course, reveals definitively the foolish-
ness of all quests for a salvation purely of this world.
Humanity cannot find its permanent form and shape within the temporal sequence. It is destined for a supratem-
poral end, and the material cosmos is destined with it to
a salvation outside time. As St. Irenaeus puts it clearly:
"Not only is matter susceptible of salvation but the salvation of man, the resurrection, implies the salvation of
matter." The Christian is obliged to work towards this
salvation of the entire universe. Our work is serious for
this reason. It is not merely a pastime. It is not merely
something to occupy us until the serious business of life
can be begun. It is not merely a means of sustenance for
us; it is a co-redemptive labor with Christ to save the
entire universe and to bring the cosmos to its definitive
state.[3]

In Christian literature the Last Things have too often
been discussed in an atmosphere of sadness and grief.
Too often the thought of the end of the world evokes
images of terrible catastrophies. What we should really
envision is the definitive triumph of Christ coming in His
glory to consummate the work of history and to inaugu-
rate the "new heaven and the new earth" (Apoc. xxi, 1;
17-20). For the meaning of the universe is revealed in the

resurrection of the Lord. When matter is assumed into glory we will see that destruction is not the term of this world's existence, since Christ is constantly active upon this material cosmos, turning it towards Himself and directing it towards the final destiny. Once we realize that the body of Christ is bound to this earth by the ties of matter we understand that He must be concerned with the events that take place upon this earth. He does not contemplate the immense struggle between good and evil, between grace and sin in human history, as something foreign to Himself. He constantly works within the interior of that history to guide the world away from the forces of destruction and to open it to His vivifying action of grace. His activity is always contemporary to the present scene.

This vital action of Christ extends beyond the realm of the spiritual, beyond the great empire of grace, beyond the world of the human soul. It actually extends to sub-human nature, to the material world itself. We are under-scoring here an ancient Christian truth which is sometimes in danger of being forgotten. The world in which man lives is man's natural habitat. It shared in man's fall and it must share in his redemption and victory, since man's body is inseparable from the world in which man dwells.

One of the conquests of mankind in these last decades has been the discovery and the appreciation of process, movement, evolution. This process concerns not only living organisms but also ideas and institutions. We have come to the point in history where we approach things gene-tically. The evolutionary concept of reality by no means rejects the presence of God within history but rather shows us His action as more living and closer to ourselves.

This fundamental intuition of an historic becoming casts

a new light upon the Christian redemption. If the redemption is tied up with human history and with the history of the world, then it will not attain its full dimensions until history and the world have come to their divinely appointed term. The Church is Christ Himself progressively assuming all humanity into union with Himself, and the material universe is touched by this activity and redeemed by it. Christ, who directs the evolutionary process, is the soul of the movement bearing human history towards its term, and He sculpts in time the face of God upon humanity. There is, as St. Augustine has pointed out, "one great man, the total Christ, growing through the centuries to His full stature." In this redemption, we must recall constantly that the corporal, the biological, the cosmological has its place. Biology discovers to us constantly the intimate bonds which tie man to his universe.

But man by his fault had drawn this universe after him in rebellion. The universe became by the sin of Adam a sort of conspirator with man, linked with him in his sin, victim of a slavery to which the sinner had reduced it. But if the universe is linked with man in his fall, it will also be linked with him in his resurrection. The Prophets announce that in the Messianic times there will be a restoration of the universe. Isaias has told us that God will create new skies and a new earth where one will no longer remember the past. St. John recalls to us that Christ renews all things and that He has introduced a germ of renewal and of transformation into earth and heaven. St. Paul places the universe solidly in the center of the redemptive activity of Christ: "Not that I count these present sufferings as the measure of that glory which is to be revealed in us. If creation is full of expectancy, that is because it is waiting for the sons of God to be made known. Created nature has been condemned to frustration; not for some deliberate fault of its own, but for the sake of him who so condemned it, with a hope to look forward to; namely, that nature in its turn will be set free from the tyranny of corruption, to share in the glorious freedom of God's sons. The whole of creation, as we know, groans in a common travail all the while" (Rom. viii, 18-22).

Here the prophetic spirit seizes St. Paul, and his vision embraces the whole of creaturedom. All inanimate nature, he tells us, aspires in its own fashion to that glorious revelation which will manifest the sons of God in their true dignity. For inanimate nature has been made subject to vanity. This was not her first state, for in the Garden of Eden nature was transfigured with glory. The earth then produced no thorns and brambles and was not yet cursed by God (Gen. vii, 17-19). Nor was it nature's own will, but the will of man, whose free rebellion against God produced this decline. But creation has retained hope; one day it will be liberated from corruption and will share in the liberty of the children of God. Now the sufferings and the corruption that we see about us are like the sighs and groans of childbirth: the world is giving birth to the new earth and those new heavens springing up since the resurrection of Christ and destined for completion at the end of time.

St. Paul's vision is that of a mystic and a poet. He knows that man is not the only one who sighs with a sense of incompleteness and sorrow. The entire creation mourns with us and awaits redemption. The universe is waiting. There is an element in it that somehow corresponds to our hope: it awaits its transfiguration and is at present charged with expectancy. Our faith in the risen Christ is the ground of our own hope and the hope of all creation.

St. John Chrysostom and St. Thomas think that the vanity to which creation has been made subject is the law of change and death. Other exegetes believe that St. Paul is referring here to the evil use that man has made of nature and creatures since the Fall. But in either case St. Paul expounds the belief that this sensible world will be restored to its primitive glory.[4]

This belief was held as certain by early Christians. Nature herself, they were sure, will be renewed and will share in her own fashion in the glory of the children of God. As long as man is under the reign of sin, nature lacks perfect order, although this is apparent not to scientific but to religious reflection. Creation, morally associated with the destiny of man, is under the sign of corruption. The image which St. Paul uses is very striking. He does not merely say that creation waits with anxiety, but that the eager expectation of creation awaits with impatience, an even bolder image.

The creation under discussion is clearly distinguished from rational creation, and it awaits its salvation, not directly, but as a result of the manifestation of the glory of the children of God. Since the sin of Adam nature itself suffers a sort of violence and is restrained from the free development of which it is capable. But since to man's condemnation in the Garden of Eden God added the hope of redemption, so creation too has its hope. When man is in the glory of the children of God, nature will recover its proper liberty. It will be delivered from the slavery to corruption and death to which it is now submitted.

In this new world mankind will visit again the scenes of its triumph and will contemplate them with joy. Human eyes need human sights to gladden them, and we can scarcely doubt that there is some deep nostalgia in the soul for that lost Eden where the lamb lay down with the lion. In the resurrected universe all the earth will support the joy of the resurrected man. This is necessary if the Incarnate Christ, the living God who pitched His tent among us, is to be shown forth as the crown of all creation. Even unthinking matter will be called upon to glorify Him, and He will assume the place that is His as the center of the world. Our human life is linked to this world, the scene of our history and labors, and it has also been the scene of Christ's activity. No rock, no blade of grass but has been changed by the fact that Christ walked this earth and drank from its springs. The aspirations of the entire world will be fulfilled in Christ, and we collaborate with Him in bringing that about. All of nature must share in that final reconciliation and all human consciousness will tend to union in the human consciousness of Christ. The world will be the completion of His humanity and our humanity, for the world and the Christian form a unit.

A whole group of sciences which have studied the history of life invite us to conceive the universe as an immense living being mounting progressively towards an ever more perfect organization, towards humanity itself, and Genesis for its part reveals the religious truth that the creative work of God found its vital fulfillment in man, its director. Man is called upon by God consciously and freely to order all creation towards Him.

This solidarity of all creation with humankind is most evident in the curse which God put upon the earth after

the Fall of Adam and Eve. This primeval fall ruptured
the harmony established by God and in place of finding
himself the central figure on earth directing all things to
God and himself directed to God, man finds himself in
a state of conflict with the world. Breaking with God, he
has interrupted the movement of all things towards God.
The material body of man is, because of this sin, no longer
perfectly submissive to the soul. Creation has become
opaque, it no longer reveals God in the fashion that it did
to Adam and Eve.

But Christ fulfills the role of redeemer, and the theater
of His redemptive operation is the entire universe, which
feels repercussion of this redemption. At the moment of
the second coming of Christ when the Savior will appear
in all His glory, the material universe will suffer a cata-
clysm, but it will be the prelude to a renewal. At the
moment of the death of the Savior this universe too
shuddered and trembled. God, who has wished to recon-
cile all things with Himself in Christ, has not neglected
to prolong this reconciliation in the material universe.
He has restored that ascending process of creatures towards God, He has given a head to the column of creaturedom mounting towards God. Creation was originally intended to be an image of God and to reveal His face to
the beholder. In the resurrected universe the presence of
Christ will be sensible in all things, even the most material.
His contact with the lowliest elements in this universe of
ours has sanctified them and begun their redemption.

In a certain sense, the miracles of Jesus during His life
in this world are a sign of His restoring, redemptive activity at work in a sensible world. When Jesus cures the
paralytic to prove His power to purify the soul He allows

matter to enter into His salvific plans. The resurrection of Lazarus is a sign of Jesus' own corporal resurrection, and by it material, created reality is permitted to reveal its deeper mystical significance. When St. Matthew describes the cosmic repercussions of Jesus' death he is only giving an illustration of the universal prolongation of Christ's redemptive death upon inanimate creation. The writers of the East—Gregory of Nyssa, for instance, and Maximus the Confessor—celebrate the action of the Eternal Word in creation and emphasize His cosmic functions.

Regenerated humanity after the resurrection will regenerate the universe, and the glory of the sons of God will shine in the entire creation. This work is the work of resurrected man and presupposes the reflection and effort of each generation in the life of the Church. The culture of each century enlarging the horizons of our knowledge permits those generations to deepen their faith and to advance this redemption of the universe. But in the last analysis it will be the transforming power of Christ which will call into being a new heaven and a new earth, this time hospitable to risen humanity, His members.

# NOTES

## I: LIFE, LAW AND LOVE

1. Cf. Yves de Montcheuil, *Mélanges Théologiques* (Paris, Aubier, 1944), pp. 354 ff.
2. S. Lyonnet, "Libérté Chrétienne et Loi Nouvelle" (Rome, Biblical Institute, 1953).

## II: SIN

1. A. George, "Le sens du Péché dans l'Ancien Testament" in *Lumière et Vie*, n. 15, pp. 21-40.
2. S. Lyonnet, *Theologia Biblica Novi Testamenti, De Peccato et Redemptione* (Rome, Biblical Institute, 1956), pp. 64-65.
3. H. Rondet, *Une Théologie du Péché* (Paris, Lethielleux, 1957), pp. 33-39.
4. *Ibid.*, p. 26.
5. The following several paragraphs are inspired by the illuminating essay of Michael Mason, "The God of Wrath and the *Mysterious Tremendum*," in *Love and Violence* (New York and London, Sheed and Ward, 1954).

## III: DEATH

1. Martin Heidegger, *Sein und Zeit* (Tübingen, Neimeyer, 1955), pp. 236-241.
2. H.-M. Féret, O.P., gives a clear synthesis of biblical traditions

on death in "La Mort dans la Tradition Biblique," *Le Mystère de la Mort et sa Célébration* (Paris, Editions du Cerf, 1951).

3. Cf. Jean Daniélou, S.J., "La Doctrine de la Mort Chez les Pères de l'Eglise," *Mystère de la Mort*, p. 160.

4. On the final option theory one can consult Emile Mersch, *Theology of the Mystical Body* (St. Louis, Herder, 1952), pp. 262 ff.; H. Rondet, S.J., Problèmes pour la Réflexion Chrétienne (Paris, Spes, 1945), pp. 149 ff.; and the articles of Peter Gumpel, S.J., in the *Downside Review*, 1954-1955.

## V: REDEMPTIVE SUFFERING

1. B. Bartmann in his *Purgatory* (London, Burns, Oates and Washbourne) has traced the development of this doctrine and clarified many misunderstandings concerning purgatory.

## VI: HELL

1. Henri Rondet, S.J., *Problèmes pour la Réflexion Chrétienne* (Paris, Spes, 1945), pp. 119-120.

2. Henri de Lubac, S.J., *Sur les Chemins de Dieu* (Paris, Aubier, 1956), p. 187.

## VII: RESURRECTION

1. Romano Guardini has suggested many insights into the nature of the risen body in the chapter "The Spiritual Body" in *The Last Things* (New York, Pantheon, 1954). See also K. Rahner, S.J., *Schriften zur Theologie* (Einsiedeln, 1955), t. 2, p. 93.

## VIII: HEAVEN

1. A. Michel, *Les Mystères de l'Au-delà* (Paris, Tequi, 1953), pp. 120-122.

2. Y. de Montcheuil, *Leçons sur le Christ* (Paris, Editions de l'Epi, 1944); Ch. XII develops this theme. This citation from Father de Montcheuil does not, of course, imply agreement with all the opinions expressed in this work, some of which have been questioned by able theologians.

3. A. Hamman, *Mystère du Salut* (Paris, Plon, 1954), pp. 201-209.

4. M.-J. Lagrange, *Epître aux Romains* (Paris, Gabalda, 1950), pp. 204-209.

## Date Due

| | | | |
|---|---|---|---|
| MAR 9 '59 | NOV 21 '62 | JY 5 '66 | |
| JUN 22 '59 | JAN 28 '63 | JY 2 6 '66 | |
| AUG 4 '59 | FEB 20 '63 | JA15'70 | |
| AUG 4 '59 | JUN 18 '63 | Ja 30 7 b | |
| FEB 1 '60 | JUL 3 '63 | AP 10'70 | |
| SE 28'60 | JY 15 '63 | | |
| OC 31'60 | JUL 31 '63 | | |
| FE 6 '61 | AUG 14 '63 | | |
| MY 3 '61 | OCT 25 '63 | | |
| JUN 20 P.M. | NO 18 '63 | | |
| JY 8 '61 | MR 4'64 | | |
| FE 8 '62 | JY 7 '64 | | |
| FE 28'62 | FE 2 2 '65 | | |
| MR 23'62 | FE 2 '66 | | |
| JE 21'62 | FE 18 '66 | | |
| JY 7 '62 | MR 4 '66 | | |
| JY 22'62 | AP 1 3 '66 | | |
| | GE | PRINTED | IN U. S. A. |